THE HOUSE
ON THE CLIFF

Lynn Lawson

COUNTRY BOOKS

Published by Country Books
Courtyard Cottage, Little Longstone, Bakewell, Derbyshire DE45 1NN
Tel: 01629 640670
e-mail: dickrichardson@country-books.co.uk
www.countrybooks.biz

ISBN 978-1-910489-37-6

© 2016 Lynn Lawson
e-mail: splashpoint@msn.com

British Library Cataloguing in Publication Data.
A catalogue record for this book is available from the British Library.

Printed and boound in England by 4edge Ltd. Hockley, Essex. Tel: 01702 200243

DEDICATION

*This book is dedicated to the volunteers at Seaford Museum,
who keep the history of this special town alive.*

CONTENTS

CONTENTS

INTRODUCTION

One of the most distinctive features that characterises Seaford seafront is the red brick wall that stretches its way up along the edge of Seaford Head from Splash Point. First time visitors speculate that it could have belonged to a fort; more knowledgeable, long-term residents of the town will tell you that is it the boundary wall of a hotel that stood there in the 1950s.

I have lived in Seaford almost all my life and had always been curious about the origins of this building, which is visible in so many photographs of the seafront taken between 1900 and the mid-1960s. After attending the 'Seaford Rediscovered 'course at the Martello Tower in 2011 I decided to investigate further, in the hope that I would be able to unearth some useful information that could be turned into a small pamphlet for the Museum shop. My initial wish to simply 'discover more' about this building gradually evolved into a full-scale project, involving countless hours spent on the internet, at the Keep Records Centre at Falmer and of course in the archives of the Museum itself. It soon become apparent that the fascinating story of *The House on the Cliff* and the people who lived in it would not only provide an insight into the history of Seaford itself, but would also reflect the huge social change that occurred in the country as a whole during the first half of the twentieth century. The role of women in Victorian times, the history of the cinema, two world wars, the rise of package holidays for the masses – all these elements have a place in the story of the house which began as the privately owned 'Cliff Cottage' in 1897 and ended as the 'Splash Point Hotel' in the late 1950s.

The results of my investigations steadily outgrew the confines of a pamphlet, until I eventually took the decision to publish the whole story in book format. I hope that the information that I have uncovered will be of interest to others who, like me, wish to learn more about the history of this un-usual house, which stood in such a unique position, high above the town and looking out over the sea.

Lynn Lawson, October 2016
e-mail: splashpoint@msn.com

CHAPTER 1

THE FIRST OWNER –
MARIA FLEMING BAXTER 1897 – 1907

In the summer of 1897, Edward Hammond, a Lewes builder, submitted a
planning application to the recently formed Seaford Urban District
Council. The plans – beautifully drawn by London architect Arnold Mitchell
– were for a building named Cliff Cottage. In response to the request for the
'situation of the building', Mr Hammond has simply written 'on the cliff'.
And in the space provided for the name 'of the persons for whom buildings
are to be erected', he has once again written just three words – 'Mrs Fleming
Baxter'.

SEAFORD FROM EAST CLIFF

A man from the early 1900s surveys the view from the top of Seaford Head.
Cliff Cottage can be seen in the foreground of the picture.

Photographs of Seaford Head taken in the early 1900s illustrate the
striking nature of the site selected for Mrs Fleming Baxter's nine-bedroomed

'cottage'. The cluster of houses that now nestle around the base of the Head did not begin to appear until the 1920s, and in 1899 the Martello Tower was the only building between Splash Point and the Esplanade Hotel, which had opened in 1891. The photographs show Cliff Cottage standing in isolation high above Seaford, exposed to all weathers but with unrivalled views of both sea and town. So who was Mrs Fleming Baxter, this Victorian lady who chose to build her house in such a dramatic setting?

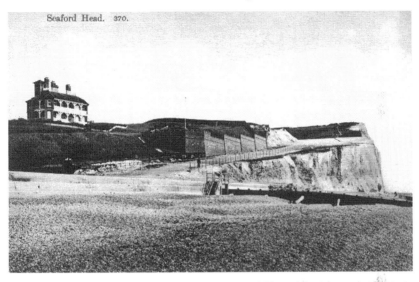

Card posted in 1913 showing the view of Cliff Cottage from the beach. The sender was one of the many people to benefit from Seaford's healthy sea air, writing 'Have been having fine weather, and feel all the better for it as I am quite well again now'.

Postcard circa 1907 showing position of Cliff Cottage.
Courtesy of the Rosemary Holland Collection

Maria Fleming Baxter – Her Background

Maria Fleming Baxter (née Hancock) was born in 1847, the eldest daughter of Charles Frederick Hancock, a well-known London jeweller. Charles was the son of a Birmingham silversmith and had risen to become a partner in Hunt and Roskell, a distinguished London firm of manufacturing and retail jewellers. Maria had evidently been born into a family of craftsmen, for her mother, Maria Edington, was the daughter of London goldsmith, John James Edington.

Maria's birth directly preceded a time of rapid change in her father's business. On 1ST January 1849 Charles founded a new company, opening a shop on the corner of Bruton Street, New Bond Street, London. Success came quickly, and only eight months after opening, 'Hancocks' the jewellers received the Royal Warrant from Queen Victoria, and she and many of the Principal Sovereigns in Europe became regular patrons. In 1856, when Maria was nine years old, Charles' company was awarded the prestigious task of producing the newly instigated Victoria Cross – the highest military decoration awarded for valour 'in the face of the enemy' – which is still made by Hancocks to this day.

Charles Frederick Hancock, famous London jeweller and father of Maria.
Photograph reproduced with kind permission of Hancocks of London www.hancockslondon.com

Maria Fleming Baxter – Her Marriage

Acccording to the 1861 census, fourteen-year-old Maria is registered as living with her parents at 39 Bruton Street, but by the time of the next census in 1871 her life had changed considerably, for she was now – at the age of twenty-four – a married woman and the mother of two small daughters. Her husband was Herbert Fleming Baxter, whose family owned Sibdon Castle, a country house in Shropshire. The census describes Herbert's occupation as an 'American Merchant' – a profitable line of business which at one point included a partnership with Alfred Clayton Cole, a future governor of the Bank of England.[1] A shipment record dating from September 1876 and signed by Herbert reveals that he and his partners were the owners of '10 cases of Turkey opium' being transported to the port of Philadelphia.[2] The idea of trading in opium was perfectly acceptable at the time, as derivatives from the drug were often sold for medicinal purposes, the most popular being Laudanum which was widely used in Victorian households as a painkiller.

Watercolour of Sibdon Castle (home of Herbert Fleming Baxter) painted by John Homes Smith in 1856, nine years before Herbert married Maria.
With kind permission of the Shropshire Archaeological and Historical Society

Herbert and Maria married at St George's Hanover Square on 27TH April 1865 and Maria moved into Herbert's London house at 2 St John's Wood Park. They were still living at this address at the time of the 1881 census, along with their two daughters – fourteen-year-old Violet and ten-year-old May – and son Fane, who had been born in 1873. By this time however the Fleming

---

[1]   The London Gazette of July 4TH 1899 reports that that this partnership of 'Commission Merchants and Bankers' had been dissolved by mutual consent.

[2]   The details of the document, which was being sold, were listed on the website of Globe Treasures .

Baxters had made the decision to move their family to a new home, and plans were underway to build a grand house in Fitzjohns Avenue, Hampsted – an area that in 1883 was claimed by Harper's Magazine to be 'one of the noblest streets in the world.'

There appears to have been no shortage of money, for the new house had twenty-five rooms, and when it was sold in 1907 was described as being

'exceptionally well built and sumptuously fitted, the woodwork being mostly of oak and polished pine…approached by a carriage sweep… the grounds are well laid out with tennis and croquet lawns, borders and shrubberies…the whole property extending to over three quarters of an acre.'[3]

Architect's drawing of 'The Tower', Fitzjohns Avenue, Hampstead –
built for the Fleming Baxters circa 1881.
Illustration courtesy of   http://www.hampsteadheath.net.

A history of Hampstead written in 1889 provides a list of houses in the parish that are assessed 'at a gross value of £400 and upwards', and the name of Herbert Fleming Baxter, 55 Fitzjohns Avenue is included in this group of wealthy and distinguished residents.[4] In the paragraph entitled 'New and

---

[3]   Advert from *The Times* May 18TH 1907, when the house was being sold after the death
        of Maria Fleming Baxter. The house still exists today and is a listed building,
        now divided into flats.

[4]   *Records of the Manor, Parish and Borough of Hampstead to December 31ST 1889 ,*
        edited by F E Baines (p81).

Considerable Houses', the author singles out Fitzjohns Avenue as having been especially enriched by the large number of beautiful and expensive homes that had been built in Hampstead during the previous thirty years. The Fleming Baxters had chosen to place themselves in one of the most desirable streets in London, with neighbours that included 'Lloyds underwriters, auctioneers, silk manufacturers, a wine merchant, a director of Hull Docks, an Arctic explorer, and an Islamic scholar',[5] as well as successful artists such as Edwin Long, Frank Holl and John Pettie.

Miniature portrait of Maria Fleming Baxter, first owner of Cliff Cottage.
According to professional dress historian Jayne Shrimpton, Maria is dressed
in 'fancy dress' costume suggesting the styles of the past.
(See Appendix 1 for further details.)
Reproduced with kind permission of Teresa Sladen

---

[5]   *A History of the County of Middlesex* Volume 9. Originally published by Victoria County History, London, 1989.

Photograph of Maria Fleming Baxter with daughters Violet (standing) and May (sitting) circa 1871.
Reproduced with kind permission of Teresa Sladen

Further information regarding the clothes worn by Maria and her daughters can be found in Appendix 1, an analysis of the photograph provided by Jayne Shrimpton (Professional dress historian and picture specialist)

Maria Fleming Baxter – Her Life in London

Maria may have been a wealthy lady from a privileged background, but excerpts from newspapers of the time reveal that she was not a woman who was content to sit at home with her sewing. We learn from the *Manchester Times*,[6] for example, that she was the 'honorary secretary' for an organisation called the Somerville Club, an association for women formed around 1880. Women from all classes were encouraged to gather at the club's premises in Oxford Street London, where they could socialise, visit the reading room, and attend regular lectures on social and political subjects with titles such as 'Some of the Uses for Clubs for Women', 'The Idiosyncrasies and Training of Babies', 'Buddhism', 'Robert Browning as a Teacher of the Nineteenth Century' and 'The Place of Women in Practical Politics.' Given the rise in demand for women's suffrage in the late 1800s it is not surprising to see politics included as a subject for discussion, and a rather flippant report in the *Manchester Courier* suggests that 'squabbling' occurred during the AGM of 1892 when a section of the membership wanted to 'extend the aegis of the club to Hyde Park demonstrations.' According to the report, the Progressives were defeated and a less militant committee then appointed. Whether Maria was still a member of the committee at this time is unknown, but her presence at the unveiling of The Women's Fawcett Memorial in 1886 – erected in memory of Henry Fawcett, a blind Liberal MP who campaigned for women's suffrage – would seem to suggest that women's rights was a subject that she cared about.[7]

The Somerville Club was not the only organisation to which Mrs Fleming

---

THE SOMERVILLE CLUB,

231, Oxford Street, is a useful club; it is opposite Peter Robinson's. The subscription is ten shillings, and the entrance fee is the same amount. The Somerville includes women of all views among its members identified with no particular party. This modest little club does not pretend to be smart or fashionable. It affords a quiet room for writing, a light, pleasant sitting-room, with comfortable easy chairs, an inexpensive luncheon, plenty of magazines and papers for the many women workers thankful for the quiet rest a club of this kind offers.

From an article on 'Ladies Clubs in London' published by The Sketch on May 16th 1894.
Maria Fleming Baxter was Hon. Sec for this organisation.

---

[6] *The Manchester Times*, Saturday 21ST April 1888.

[7] The writer of 'Our Ladies Column' in *The Western Times* of Monday 9TH August names 'Mrs Fleming Baxter' as one of the people seen at this event. The memorial is in the Embankment Gardens and the words underneath read 'Erected to the memory of Henry Fawcett by his grateful countrywomen'.

Baxter belonged. She was also a member of the National Health Society, which was founded in 1871 by Elizabeth Blackwell, the first woman to receive a medical degree in the United States. The aim of this society was to prevent ill health by promoting education on health and hygiene – under the slogan 'Prevention is better than Cure' – and lectures were delivered on subjects such as 'Compulsory Vaccination', 'Health in the House' and 'Wholesome Food'.

Maria's role in this society included hosting events at The Tower – the family's London home – and the *York Herald* of January 1891 reports that Queen Victoria's surgeon Sir Spencer Wells presided at a 'largely attended drawing room meeting held under the auspices of the National Health Society, at the residence of Mrs Fleming Baxter, Fitzjohns Avenue, with the view of establishing in Hampstead a class for the hygienic education of woman.'[8] This meeting was addressed by various other speakers, one of them being Mrs Fleming Baxter herself.[9]

As well as organising lectures, the National Health Society also produced pamphlets which provided advice on a range of health-related subjects. The *Bristol Mercury* of 28th February 1891 refers to one such pamphlet 'written by a lady' and called 'How to be Strong and Beautiful'.[10] The columnist suggests that readers 'who care about the questions of sensible clothing' should send three stamps to get themselves a copy of this useful publication. Women were now beginning to rebel against the restrictive dress of the time – such as heavy skirts and tightly fitting corsets – and there were various attempts to promote more comfortable options that would provide greater freedom of movement and allow them to participate in sporting activities such as cycling or golf. In 1884 Maria herself had modelled one such alternative at the International Health Exhibition which was held in South Kensington – a Highland or 'mountaineering' costume, made of dark blue cloth with 'gaiters, knickerbockers, a skirt reaching to the knees, and a very pretty short coat like a gentleman's shooting jacket.'[11]

[8]   *The York Herald* of Monday 12TH January 1891. Sir Thomas Spencer Wells was an eminent gynaecological surgeon who also lived in Hampstead, in a house called Golders Hill.

[9]   Mrs Fleming Baxter was still a member of the Society seven years later in 1898, as the *Morning Post* of 29TH March reports that she was present at the society's AGM.

[10]   'Our Ladies Column' in the *Bristol Mercury*, Saturday 28TH February 1891.

[11]   *The Science of Dress in Theory and Practice* by Ada S Ballin (1885). The clothing section in the Exhibition Catalogue lists exhibit number 323 as 'A lady's costume for the Highlands'. (Exhibited by Mrs H F Baxter, The Tower, Hampstead).

A New House by the Sea

The Tower would have provided an ideal base for the Fleming Baxters' London activities, and the family also paid regular visits to Sibdon Castle, Herbert's family home in Shropshire, which he eventually purchased from his older brother in 1899 for a price of £30,000.[12] Yet another option for a change of scene was provided by Maria's houseboat, Red Rover, based at Shiplake on the Thames and seemingly a familiar sight at Chertsey.[13] Then, in the late 1890s, when Maria was fifty, she decided to build another house, this time by the sea, in the small Sussex town of Seaford.

So why Seaford? A guide book from 1890[14] emphasises the appeal of this 'snug little town' in comparison with more fashionable watering places. The author, W Banks, relates how he faithfully visits Seaford each summer, attracted by the 'quiet of a seaside village' that 'does not boast of any grand buildings, squares or terraces calculated to impress the visitor with an exalted sense of its importance'. There is no 'clamorous cab stand' or an 'array of omnibuses with open doors and noisy conductors' waiting to assault him at the railway station, but instead a 'good substantial carriage of somewhat doubtful style and age, drawn by a steady going horse'.

The railway had reached Seaford in 1864, and Mr Banks enthuses over the sights to be viewed from the train window:

> 'As we whirl along this bright summer afternoon I can see the sky, the sea, the beach, the snug little village of Blatchington peeping from amidst a group of elms on the extreme left. …seaward it is dead low water; the smooth ocean lies breathing in the sunlight…only the tiniest of waves curl over the shingle'.

The presence of the sea would undoubtedly have played an important part in the selection of the town of Seaford as the location for Mrs Fleming Baxter's new house. There was much talk in Victorian times of the beneficial effect of sea air on health, and several convalescent homes were built in Seaford between 1870 and 1901. It is possible therefore that Maria's association with the National Health Society brought the town to her attention. In 1876 the *Magazine of Pharmacy* published an article entitled 'Seaford as a Health Resort',[15] in which we learn that one of the doctors to send patients to recover

---

[12] From an article on Sibdon Castle published in *Country Life* magazine June 1967.

[13] *The Pall Mall Gazette* of Monday 20TH June 1892 prints an article about Maria's daughter, May, whom it claims was a model for a character in JM Barrie's play *Walker London*, which is set on a houseboat. The article refers to 'Miss M Fleming Baxter, one of the Senior Optimes in the Mathematical Tripos at Cambridge …whose mother's house boat, Red Rover, is well known at Chertsey.'

[14] W Banks *Seaford Past and Present. Handbook and Visitor Guide 1890-91.*

[15] *The Hastings and St Leonard's Observer* of 24TH June 1876.

11

in the town of Seaford was none other than Mr Spencer Wells, the surgeon who was later to address the meeting held in Mrs Fleming Baxter's drawing room.

from London. The cost of living at Seaford, the writer contends, is not more than usual for a watering place, although he hints that some allowance must be made for the enormous appetite which the air of Seaford soon engenders. Coming to the specific complaints for which the air is beneficial he says: "Seaford is eminently suitable to persons recovering from the weaknesses consequent on surgical operations. Mr. Spencer Wells sends many of his patients to this town. Diseases of the brain and nervous system, bronchitis, dyspepsia, erysipelas, fevers and inflammations, female complaints, disease of the kidney, rheumatism, syphilis, debility and more especially nervous debility, may be all benefited by the air and climate of Seaford." Speaking of the fearful storm which

In June 1876 the Hastings and St Leonards Observer published an item entitled 'Seaford as Health Resort' which discussed an article on this subject that had appeared in the Magazine of Pharmacy. The above extract lists a wide range of ailments that could allegedly benefit from 'the air and climate of Seaford'. Mr Spencer Wells – the surgeon referred to in the article – was later to address a meeting of the National Health Society in Maria Fleming Baxter's drawing room, and could therefore have introduced her to the town.

11 SEAFORD. — The Esplanade. — Looking West. — LL.

Seaford seafront looking west circa 1909. The message on the back reads 'When the sea is very rough it goes right over the road into the basement of these hotels. There are none of these boats on the beach now. They are all pulled up in a line along the gutters.'

Seaford seafront looking east, with Cliff Cottage just visible in the background. The sender, who posted the card in 1905, wrote 'People say this is a pretty place. Wind blowing every day.'

The sender of this early card of sailing boats on the beach – posted in 1904 – has written the simple message 'On the Seaford beach' on the front, using the space on the reverse for the address only. The 1898 edition of Black's Guide to Sussex and its Watering Places lists Seaford's attractions as 'an esplanade, a shingly beach, bathing machines, rowing boats, sailing yachts and cricket field'.[16]

---

[16] *Black's Guide to Sussex and its Watering Places*, eleventh edition, published by Adam and Charles Black, London 1898.

A further attraction for a lady with an interest in healthy living could have been the proximity of the recently-opened golf course on Seaford Head, where Seaford Ladies Golf Club had been established in April 1895. According to John Walsh's book 'Seaford Golf Club – A History', the course for ladies was 'a nine hole one, but of a distinctly sporting character... and by no means easy'[17] – just the sort of challenge that could have appealed to a woman like Maria.

Postcard of Seaford Golf Links showing the prominent position of Cliff Cottage. Not everyone enjoyed their stay in Seaford, for the sender of this card, posted in 1913, writes: 'This is a very slow place. I shall be glad to leave it'.

The 'lady's costume for the Highlands' which Mrs Fleming Baxter had modelled at the International Health Exhibition was designed for women who enjoyed invigorating walks in the countryside, and a house on Seaford Head would certainly have provided an ideal base for anyone wishing to explore the Sussex Downs on foot. The section on 'Walks and Drives' in the 1890 *Visitors' Guide* encourages the reader to take the footpath past Millberg College (now Corsica Hall) on to the Downs, where he will behold

> 'one of the most charming scenes on the southern coast...the bay, with its sweep of several miles, in various phases of ocean calm and billow...the opposite cliffs of Newhaven....the low lands in the fore-ground, flanked by the cheerful looking town with its old grey church in the middle distance.'

---

[17]   From *Golf* July 9TH 1895 as quoted in *Seaford Golf Club A History* by John H Walsh pub by Lindel Publicity and Promotions Ltd 1986.

Seaford from the Downs, posted in May 1906. The sender writes 'I have just been enjoying a walk along the front. It is lovely and warm enough to sit on the beach.'

Another postcard posted in 1906 showing the view of the town from Seaford Head, with the roof and top floor of Cliff Cottage just visible in the picture.

Seaford Bay 17

The top of Seaford Head has always been a popular place from which to admire the views of the town and the bay (postcard pre-1910)

The author could have been standing on the site of Maria's future house, but we do not need to rely on descriptions from guidebooks to remind us of the stunning location of Cliff Cottage. In 1907 Maria's sister wrote the following message on a postcard to an unknown recipient:

'This is my sister's house, where we are now staying. Overlooking the beach and right on the Downs – as I sit at the window it is lovely – and for a wonder today is very clear and fine. One can see nearly 40 miles off. Over to France. You would love it all.'

Cliff Cottage . July . Aug - 07.

6   SEAFORD. — *The Cliffs and Downs.* — LL.

Postcard showing Cliff Cottage in the early years of the twentieth century.
The words were written by Maria's sister who was staying in the house during the summer of 1907
(see reverse of postcard for full message).

POST CARD.

This space may be used for correspondence
(Post office Regulation).

The address to be written here.

Inland ½ d.
Foreign 1 d.
Printed in
France

This is my sister's house – where we are now staying – over looking the beach and right on the downs – as I sit at the window it is lovely. – & for a wonder to-day is very clear & fine – One can see nearly 4 o'miles off – over to France – You will love it all.

The Architect – Arnold Mitchell

The man chosen by Maria to design her new house was esteemed architect Arnold Bidlake Mitchell, who had begun practice in 1886, specialising in parish halls, houses and schools. Mitchell's entry in the *Oxford Dictionary of Architecture and Landscaping* describes him as a gifted Arts and Crafts architect, and notes how he was responsible for designing various significant buildings during the Edwardian era, including St Felix School, Southwold Suffolk (1902) and University College School, Hampstead (1905 –7).

In 1897 Mitchell designed Westover Hall, a luxurious family home in Milford on Sea, for wealthy German industrialist Alexander Siemens, who brought the first electricity to the UK. This was a bigger house than Cliff Cottage but the two projects shared certain similarities – both houses were built around the same date, both were constructed of red brick with tile hung façades, and both were located in small coastal towns with views of the sea from their windows.

Architectural historian Clare Sherriff notes how the Westover Hall commission was an important break for the young architect 'introducing him to a new utility industrialist and also to a continental family'.[18] She describes Mitchell as 'an individualist ... who sought out the magic of site' – an interesting observation on an architect whose early projects were to include Cliff Cottage, with its spectacular views of both the Sussex Downs and the English Channel. Arnold Mitchell later added many other famous names to his list of clients including the King of Belgium, Ernest Cassell (a friend of Edward VII) and the Cook family, owners of Thomas Cook travel agents. He was also celebrated as the designer of Lott's Building Bricks for children, launched at the 1918 British Industries Fair, where Queen Mary was the first customer.

[18]   *Arnold Mitchell (1863-1944) Fecundity and Versatility in an Early Twentieth-Century Architect* by Clare Sherriff 2012.

Lott's Building Bricks were designed by architect Arnold Mitchell who also drew the plans for Cliff Cottage. The bricks are made of stone and can be used to create a variety of buildings including houses, schools and churches.

Illustration courtesy of Grace's Guide to British Industrial History website
http://www.gracesguide.co.uk/

Westover Hall in Milford on Sea, originally a private house designed by
Arnold Mitchell for Alexander Siemens in 1897. The property is currently a hotel
called The Beach House, and is now a Grade 2 listed building.

The Builder – Edward Hammond

Maria had selected a well-known London architect to design her cottage, but the builder, Edward Hammond, was a local man. Edward was born in Lewes in 1863, and by the time of the census of 1881 was already working as an architect's clerk, progressing to clerk-surveyor by 1891. Archives at The Keep Records Centre hold details of several planning applications submitted by 'Edward Hammond, builder' during the 1890s, including the plans for The Croft, Rotten Row, a house he built in 1899 for the owner of the Phoenix Foundry, John Henry Every.

Edward had worked in partnership with Lewes surveyor Henry Curtis Card, but in 1898 the *London Gazette* reported that the arrangement between the two parties had been 'terminated and dissolved by mutual consent'[19]. It is interesting to note that in June 1896 Henry Card and Son had submitted plans to build a house called 'Barons Down' in Brighton Road, Lewes – for the architect who designed this building was none other than Arnold B Mitchell. The partnership that existed between the Card family and Edward Hammond suggests that he could have worked with Arnold Mitchell on this project, leading to their collaboration on the building of Cliff Cottage two years later.[20]

---

[19] *London Gazette* of October 7TH 1898.

[20] Edward Hammond continued to work on numerous building projects in Lewes until his death in 1929. His obituary in the *Sussex Express* refers to him as 'the well-known Lewes builder' with a 'retiring disposition'.

The House is Built

In the planning application Edward Hammond describes Cliff Cottage as being 'brick built and tiled', and tinted postcards of the time show that the roof was red. Early photographs portray the house as being predominantly white in colour; this was due to the decorative woodwork that Arnold Mitchell had added to the verandas that were a feature of both the ground and the first floor on three sides of the building.

The above postcard from the early 1900s shows the view of Cliff Cottage from Seaford College (then a private school but now Corsica Hall). The house on the left is Ellenbank, which was demolished relatively recently. The photograph below provides a present day perspective of the same view, taken from Corsica Hall.

Reproduced with kind permission of Phillip Mann Estate Agents

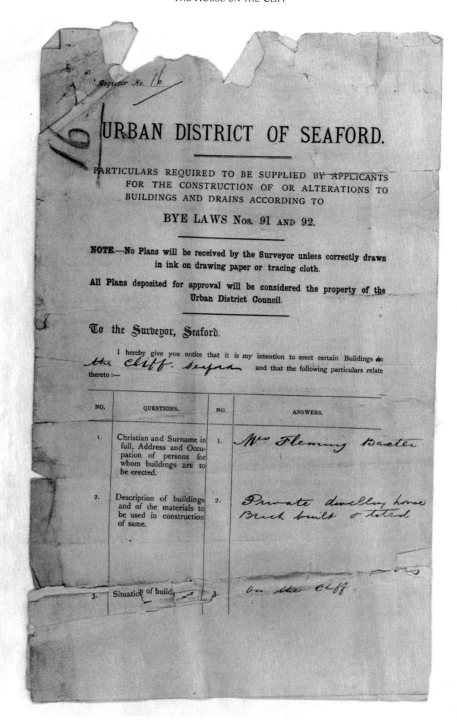

First page of planning application for Cliff Cottage submitted by builder Edward Hammond in July 1897.

East Sussex Records Office DL/A34/16

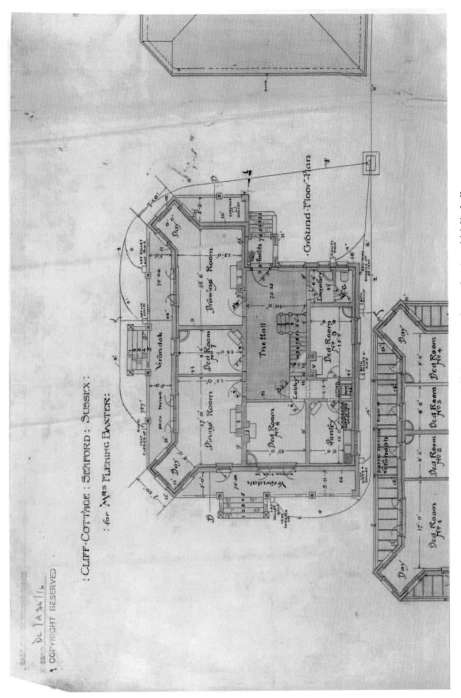

Ground floor plan for Cliff Cottage, as drawn by Arnold Mitchell.
East Sussex Records Office DL/A34/16

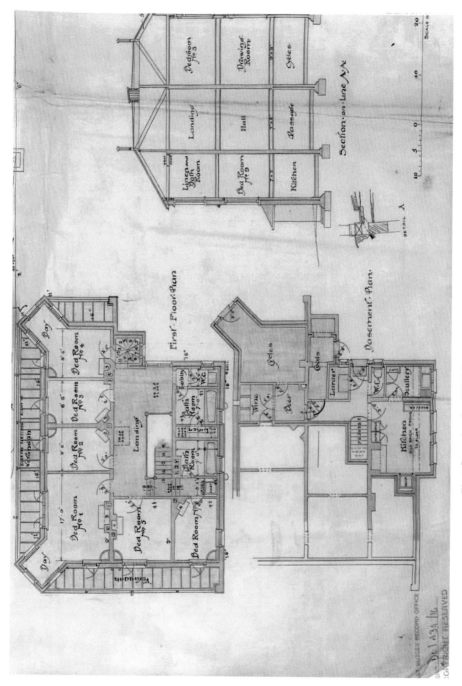

First floor plan for Cliff 'Cottage', which had nine bedrooms.
East Sussex Records Office DL/A34/16

New kitchen arrangements for Cliff Cottage, showing the name of Arnold Mitchell, the well-known Arts and Crafts architect who designed Cliff Cottage
East Sussex Records Office DL/A34/16

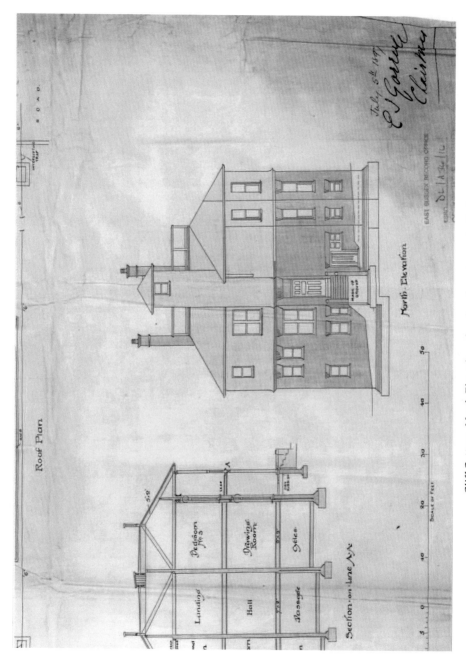

Cliff Cottage, North Elevation, showing the entrance to the house
East Sussex Records Office DL/A34/16

The house had three floors: a ground floor, first floor and also a basement, which provided storage rooms for wine, beer, coals and cycles. There were nine bedrooms – three on the ground floor and six on the first floor – but only two bathrooms, something that would be inconceivable in a house of this size today. The ground floor plan shows steps leading to an entrance hall; on the right hand side of the hall were three doors – the first leading to an eighteen-foot drawing room, the second to a small bedroom and the third to a seven-teen-foot dining room. The rooms on this side of the house all faced the sea, and the dining room and drawing room both had doors that opened onto a long veranda, as well as bays set into their corners. This layout was repeated upstairs, for identical bays were incorporated into two of the six bedrooms on the first floor, which also had a veranda running along the length of the building. Arnold Mitchell wished to ensure that the inhabitants of Cliff Cottage would be able to make the most of the sea views, for he added a narrow tower with a staircase and windows, which can be seen rising from the roof beside the chimneys. If the Fleming Baxters were in residence on February 8TH 1899 they may have watched the Danish barque Peruvian being torn apart by the waves after it ran aground opposite the Esplanade Hotel; they would have had even better views of the Norwegian ship Sagatun which was wrecked between the Head and the Martello Tower in September 1900.

Postcard posted in 1908. Cliff Cottage can be seen in the background behind the two cyclists. Arnold Mitchell's plans included a basement to be used for the storage of 'wine, beer, coals and cycles', which reflected the boom in cycling that had occurred in the 1890s.

The wreck of the Norwegian barque Sagatun , which became stranded on Seaford beach while trying to reach Newhaven Harbour on September 24TH 1900. The brick wall of Cliff Cottage can be seen in the background of the picture.
Courtesy of Seaford Museum

The House – Inhabited at Last

In the summer of 1899 the Fleming Baxters announced the marriage of their daughter, May, to John Fawcett, a physician at Guys Hospital. The announcement, published in the *Morning Post* of Wednesday 19TH July, refers to May as the 'younger daughter of Herbert Fleming Baxter, The Tower, Fitzjohns Avenue, Hampstead, Cliff Cottage, Seaford, and Houseboat Red Rover, Shiplake'. The house was now complete, and the Fleming Baxters proud to proclaim ownership.

We can only speculate as to which members of the Fleming Baxter family visited Cliff Cottage, or how much time they spent there. In 1903 it provided the honeymoon location for Herbert's niece Constance Clissold and her new husband Captain Gilbert Bailey, the house having been 'kindly lent by Mrs Fleming Baxter.'[21] When the census of 1901 was carried out, Maria and Herbert were at the Hampstead house, together with five servants and a visitor, their solicitor and family friend Edward Freeland. Cliff Cottage was not empty however, as there were three servants in residence: fifty-eight-year-old housekeeper Emily Legget, a widow; sixteen-year-old parlour maid Violet Blake, and fifteen-year-old Lily Blake, registered as 'kitchen maid domestic'. All three servants were from London: Violet and Lily were sisters, born in Camberwell. Sadly, Violet Blake was to die in childbirth in 1912, but Lily lived until the age of eighty-seven. Her granddaughter, Janette Wells, remembers how Lily liked to talk about her time in service with the Fleming Baxters. She was based at the London house most of the time, but enjoyed

---

[21] *Leamington Spa Courier* Friday 10TH July 1903.

being sent to Seaford, where the servants would have been responsible for preparing Cliff Cottage for the arrival of members of the family.[22] Another relative recalls how Lily also travelled to Sibdon Castle, where she disliked waiting on table because a son of the house – either Maria's son Fane, or more likely one of Herbert's nephews who lived at the Castle – 'had an eye for her', a common hazard for girls in service. Violet and Lily's mother, Clara Blake (née Gould), had also worked for the Fleming Baxter family and in 1881 is registered at the St John's Wood house as 'cook' aged twenty-three. The fact that Clara's daughters were later employed in the same household suggests that a satisfactory working relationship had been established between the two families.

Maria may not have always created a favourable impression on those who knew her. Her great-granddaughter, Teresa Sladen, remembers how family hearsay portrayed her as a formidable woman who had undermined the confidence of Teresa's grandmother, Maria's younger daughter May.[23] Teresa also recalls meeting a very elderly lady who had lived at Sibdon Castle in the latter years of the nineteenth century, when Maria would have been a regular visitor. This lady was Hilda Fleming Baxter – daughter of Herbert's older brother Henry – whose name appears in the census records for Sibdon Castle in 1881 (aged four) and again in 1901 (aged twenty-four). It would appear that Hilda did not hold any affection for her aunt, for she told Teresa's mother that she didn't want to be buried anywhere near Maria in Sibdon Churchyard.

Bust of Maria Fleming Baxter created by her son Fane, a sculptor who exhibited at various galleries including the Royal Academy. Fane inherited Sibdon Estate on the death of his father, but never lived there and eventually sold it in 1929.[24] In the 1911 census he described himself as 'Artist Sculptor'.

Reproduced with kind permission of Teresa Sladen

[22]   Email from Janette Wells, granddaughter of Lily Blake, October 2013.
[23]   Email from Teresa Sladen, great-granddaughter of Maria Fleming Baxter, October 2013.
[24]   From an article on Sibdon Castle published in *Country Life* magazine June 1967.

Maria also appears to have ruffled a few feathers in Seaford, for the Seaford Urban District Council minutes of 1899 –1900 document a rather acrimonious dispute relating to the public right of way which ran 'from the Esplanade at Cliff End to the cliffs' via the grounds on the seaward side of Cliff Cottage. Maria did not want the people of Seaford to use it and closed the footpath at both ends; when the council wrote to her to complain they reported that 'she states that she does not acknowledge the rights of the public but considers the path to be her private property'. In March 1900 the council threatened to consult their solicitor if she did not remove the offending fences; presumably this had the desired effect as there is no further mention of the matter in the subsequent minutes. The ordinance survey map of 1908 shows a public footpath clearly marked near the edge of the cliff, running between the sea and the famous brick wall that still stands there today. Perhaps the wall itself was Maria's final response to the problem, and erected in order that the public would not be visible from her property and vice versa. Photographs of the time confirm that the wide chalky area between the cliff edge and the wall was indeed used as a means of accessing Seaford Head – a comparison with same view today provides a startling illustration of the effects of erosion, as this part of the cliff has almost completely disappeared.

Ordinance Survey Map from 1908 showing the location of the public footpaths (in green) running either side of Cliff Cottage. Maria Fleming Baxter attempted to prevent the public from using the path on the seaward side of her house, and probably built the brick wall that still stands there today (shown in red) in order to protect her privacy. The footpath that ran along the other side of the house was enclosed by fences on both sides, creating a narrow passageway (see photograph on p.21)

Postcard sent in 1908 showing people walking up the wide stretch of cliff beside the house.
A public footpath ran along here, and it possible that Maria built the wall
to protect the privacy of her house and grounds.

Postcard entitled 'Seaford The Cliff Walk' (circa 1916) which provides another perspective of the
public right of way which existed near the cliff edge. The wall which marks the boundary of the
grounds of Cliff Cottage is visible at the bottom of the path.

31

In August 1901 the name 'Mrs Fleming Baxter' once again appeared in the council minutes, when she was granted permission to erect steps at 'Cliff End' on the West Side of Groyne no 51. This time however there was to be no conflict; for Maria confirmed that 'the public should be allowed to use them.'

Postcard posted in 1905. The steps to the beach were erected by Maria Fleming Baxter, the first owner of Cliff Cottage.

Postcard posted in 1907, showing the steps to the beach and the wall of Cliff Cottage.

The Fleming Baxters were to have relatively little time in which to enjoy their seaside retreat. Herbert Fleming Baxter died at Sibdon Castle on 21ST July 1905 at the age of sixty-five, leaving a considerable personal estate valued at £186,676. His wife and children were well provided for, and his lengthy will includes many individual legacies to friends, family and employees, including fifty pounds to the carpenter for Sibdon Estate and twenty-five pounds to the senior gardener.

The will of MR. HERBERT FLEMING BAXTER, of The Tower, Fitzjohns Avenue, and Sibdon Castle, Salop, who died on July 21, was proved on Aug. 18 by Fane Fleming Baxter, the son, Thomas Leslie Nelson, and Edward Lionel Thornton Stilwell Freeland, the value of the real and personal estate being £186,676. The testator settles the Sibdon Castle Estate on his wife for life, with remainder to his son and his heirs male. He gives £21,000, in trust, for his wife for life, and then to his three children £20,000, in trust, for his son; £15,000, in trust, for each of his daughters, Mrs. Violet Fleming Nelson and Mrs. May Fleming Fawcett; £250 each to his sons-in-law, Thomas Leslie Nelson and Dr. John Fawcett; £200 to Edward L. T. S. Freeland; £250 each to Ethel Frances Clissold, Elizabeth Constance Clissold, and Augusta Mary Warren; and other legacies. The residue of his property he leaves to his three children.

The above item from the Illustrated London News *of September 2ND 1905 provides a useful summary of the contents of Herbert Fleming Baxter's lengthy will.*

Less than two years later, on 6TH February 1907, Maria herself died at Sibdon, aged sixty. Maria's will is shorter and more straightforward than Herbert's, and the instructions for the distribution of her £50,345 estate are simple and clear. Her son Fane was to inherit the contents of Sibdon Castle; he soon put these up for sale, eventually selling the Castle itself in 1929.[25] The contents of The Tower in Hampstead were to be divided equally between Fane and his two sisters, and only three months after Maria's death the house itself was on the market, with a new family in residence by 1908.

So what was to become of Cliff Cottage? Maria's will contain details of other property and effects which belonged to her, including 'my cottage and grounds at Seaford and contents.' Her phrasing is interesting as it reinforces the idea that the house belonged to Maria, and Maria alone.[26] The name 'Mrs Fleming Baxter' had appeared on the plans; the house was lent to the honeymoon couple by 'Mrs Fleming Baxter'; Maria's will refers firmly and clearly to '**my** cottage at Seaford' [*my emphasis*]. Her seaside retreat was not, however, destined to be passed on to her three children, whom she

---

[25]   The will of Fane Fleming Baxter's sister, Violet, who died in 1936, refers to items of furniture which she purchased 'on the sale of the effects of Sibdon Castle on the death of my mother'.

[26]   Cliff Cottage is not mentioned in Herbert Fleming Baxter's will; neither is the houseboat.

Postcard of Rough Sea Seaford (posted in 1907) with the boundary wall of Cliff Cottage showing on the left of the photograph.

The Cliffs, Seaford, postmarked 1909. The boys are wearing uniform so could be from one of the many private schools that sprang up around the town in the early 1900s.

34

LOW TIDE, SEAFORD.

This interesting photograph entitled 'Low Tide, Seaford' is undated but was almost certainly taken in the early 1900s. It provides a different perspective of Splash Point and shows the amount of sand present at the time.

considered to have been 'otherwise well provided for'.[27] Instead Cliff Cottage was to have a new owner, for Maria had instructed that the house – along with her houseboat and all her personal effects and jewellery – should now become the property of her 'old and dear friend', solicitor Edward Freeland.

27] These are Maria's own words taken from her will. They presumably allude to the provision made for them by their father, as well as the bequests made by Maria herself.

CHAPTER 2

A NEW OWNER 1907 – EDWARD LIONEL THORNTON STILWELL FREELAND

On first reading Maria Fleming Baxter's will, it seems surprising that she left Cliff Cottage to her solicitor, rather than to a member of her family. Edward Freeland, however, may well have been rather more than an 'old and dear friend'. Teresa Sladen – Maria's great-granddaughter – was told by her mother that Edward had been Maria's lover and that he had a bedroom at the London house, where he is registered as a 'visitor' in the 1901 census. Edward's legacy was indeed substantial, as Maria had instructed that he should receive:

• My houseboat and contents and the lands on the River adjoining
• My cottage and grounds at Seaford and contents
• The contents of my bedroom and drawing room at The Tower
• My own personal effects and jewellery both at Sibdon and at The Tower
• A sum of money to the extent of one third of all my other property.[28]

We may not be certain that the couple were lovers, but Maria's will reveals that Edward had undoubtedly been an important person in her life.

So what do we know of Edward Freeland, the new owner of Cliff Cottage?

Edward had been born in Chichester in 1857, the third of eleven children. The Freelands were a well-known local family and Edward's father was a surgeon, magistrate and the first Medical Officer for Chichester. Two of Edward's brothers also became doctors, but Edward followed in the footsteps of his maternal grandfather and uncle, who were both solicitors.[29] Census

---

[28] The remaining two-thirds was to be divided equally among Maria's three children, with the exception of £1,000 which was 'to be devoted to gifts to my old friends by my Executor'.

[29] Information provided by Ann Griffiths, great-niece of Edward Freeland.

records show that in 1871 he was attending Queen Elizabeth's School in Ipswich, where the author Rider Haggard was a fellow pupil. Ten years later, aged twenty-three, he was already being described as a 'solicitor', and in the 1891 census he is registered at the house of his sister, Mabel Wrottesley, who was living in Buckland Crescent in Hampstead, just a short walk from the Fleming Baxters' London home in Fitzjohns Avenue.

Whether Maria and Edward were already acquainted at the time of this census is a matter for speculation, but his professional life is easier to document than his personal life and he unquestionably became a very successful solicitor, eventually practising from Queen Anne's Gate, Westminster. A trawl through the newspaper archives from the early 1900s produces several death announcements which name Edward Freeland as the solicitor to the executors of the wills of clients with such grand names as Frederick Augustus Page – Turner, Dame Mildred Bateman Scott and Dame Algitha Maud Langrishe. Edward was often a beneficiary himself, and amongst the legacies he received were £1,500 from the Earl of Portsmouth; £100 from Lord Kitchener's lieutenant, JM Cheetham; and a generous bequest of £5,000 from Maria Fleming Baxter's daughter, Violet, on her death in 1936.[30] In 1930, Colonel Sir Henry Knolleys, who had commanded the royal artillery in Africa and had also been secretary to the Queen of Norway, left him £50 'in the token of the friendship and respect in which I have held him for the past twenty three years'. Maria and her daughter were not the only members of the Fleming Baxter family to remember Edward in their wills, for Maria's husband Herbert left him two hundred pounds 'as an acknowledgement for his trouble in undertaking the office of executor'.

The local street directories show that Edward still owned Cliff Cottage until at least 1915, eight years after Maria's death. It is likely that he too used it as a holiday/weekend home, for the 1911 census lists the occupants as thirty-five-year-old caretaker Frederick Castle and his wife Nellie. Around 1915 Edward purchased a large house in Embankment Gardens, Chelsea, which he owned until his death in 1938. By 1917 he had sold the cottage in Seaford, perhaps to help fund the purchase of this impressive London property which is now divided into flats.

Edward remains a somewhat enigmatic figure in the 'Cliff Cottage' story, as he never married and therefore has no known descendants. He died aged eighty in 1938 at 14 Chapel Street, Westminster, the home of thirty-eight-year-old Mercy Wilkinson and her 'partner' Major William Alexander Camac

---

[30] Maria's great-granddaughter tells how Violet Fleming Baxter became by far the wealthiest of Maria's three children, 'having played the stock exchange very successfully all her life'.

*23 Embankment Gardens, Chelsea, which Edward Freeland owned from around 1915
until his death in 1938.*

Reproduced with kind permission of www.idmproperties.com

Wilkinson, a highly decorated British army officer and famous cricketer.[31] Edward had dealt with many complicated and lengthy documents during his career as a solicitor but his own will is very brief, simply stating that 'I give devise and bequeath all my estate and effects whatsoever and wheresoever to my many years adopted daughter Mercy Marian Mona Wilkinson née Webbe'. Mysteriously Mercy Wilkinson's parents, Peroline and Alexander Webbe, both outlived Edward Freeland, begging the question, why did he refer to Mercy as his 'adopted daughter '? Mercy herself was to die childless only seven years later at the age of forty-five. If Maria Fleming Baxter had left behind any diaries or personal effects relating to Cliff Cottage, then regrettably they were not destined to be passed down through a family line.

---

[31]   Although Mercy took the surname of Wilkinson, this was done through deed poll rather than through marriage, probably because the Colonel already had a wife. The legal name change was announced in the *London Gazette* of 17TH July 1934 by her solicitor, who was of course Edward Freeland.

Postcard showing the Martello tower with Cliff Cottage in the background. The skating rink and tea rooms were built by Seaford resident Tom Funnell, who purchased the Tower in 1911.

Postcard dated 1912. The groynes visible in the photograph were a feature of Seaford Beach until the sea defence work of the 1980s.

Seaford from Splash Point, posted in 1913. The sender writes 'I'm here for a while –
it is a very pretty place.'

Splash Point, Seaford Cliffs. The sender – who posted the card in 1916 – was another happy visitor,
writing 'We have arrived and ought to have a nice time for it is a pretty place and the air is lovely'.

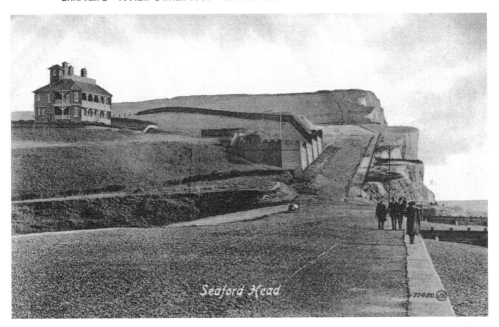

Postcard of Seaford Head showing Cliff Cottage circa 1917.

This postcard from around 1930 provides an interesting comparison with the one above.
The distinctive white woodwork which Arnold Mitchell had added to the verandas of Cliff Cottage
has disappeared, and the house now has a new dining room and 'porthole windows' which were built
by the Addinsell family in 1924. Another significant change is the appearance of the cars on the
promenade at Splash Point.

41

Another postcard of the same view (see p41), probably taken in the immediate post-war years.
Windows have now been added to the veranda on the ground floor, but the most noticeable difference
from the 1930 photograph is the increase in the number of cars on the promenade.

Courtesy of the Rosemary Holland Collection

The sender of this card – posted in August 1916 –
was staying at the Esplanade Hotel and wrote
'Having the most lovely weather and a nice time.
Dorothy is quite all right and loves bathing from the
hotel. I love Seaford and the air is A1'.

CHAPTER 3

THE FIRST WORLD WAR – RAYMOND WILLIS

When Cliff Cottage was built, Seaford was a small resort where the Victorians came to take the sea air, perhaps enjoying a stroll along the promenade or playing a round of golf at the recently opened course on Seaford Head. But by the time Edward Freeland sold the house in 1916, there were visitors of a different kind, for the town was the site of two temporary camps housing hundreds of troops destined for the battlefields of France. During this period there would have been few houses whose occupants remained untouched by the traumatic events of 1914-18, and Cliff Cottage was no exception.

The new owner of the house was Raymond Willis, a soldier who had seen active service and had been severely wounded on 13TH May 1916 while taking part in the second battle of Ypres. Like Maria and Edward before him,

Raymond came from a privileged background – his father was an insurance broker who later became the owner of Garbrand Hall, an imposing 18TH century mansion near Epsom. Raymond was educated at Haileybury before entering the firm of insurance brokers of which his father was chairman. In 1904 he went to Canada to set up a branch office,

Second Lieutenant Raymond Willis.
Unit: 5TH Reserve Cavalry Regiment,
attached to 18TH (Queen Marys Own) Hus-
sars. Death: 25 March 1918, Somme, Western
France.
Courtesy of Imperial War Museum©IWM (HU) 127627).

returning in 1910 when he was admitted as a partner in the firm and elected as a member of Lloyds.[32]

On 31ST August 1914 – immediately after the outbreak of war – Raymond joined the West Kent Yeomanry as Private 1136. His great-nephew, Nicholas Willis, has always found it quite strange that 'a young man from a very well to do family would have signed up as a trooper at the beginning of the war' and speculates that this decision could be attributed to 'how his generation felt from Rupert Brooke etc'.[33]

Raymond spent the summer of 1916 recuperating from the wounds he had received at Ypres, before returning to light duty in the autumn of that year. In January 1917 he married Emmie A Court Allan Cassells, the daughter of a Toronto barrister, whom he had presumably met whilst living in Canada. By this time Raymond Willis was listed as the occupant of Cliff Cottage, so it would appear that the house on Seaford Head was to be the somewhat un-conventional location for their first home. Perhaps this wild and windy spot provided Raymond with a suitable escape from the horrors of the trenches – his mother Charlotte, who died in 1916, had owned a house in Brunswick Terrace in Hove, so it is possible that he was familiar with the area after spending holidays there.

By 1918 Raymond had returned to the front, having become a lieutenant in the 5TH Reserve Cavalry Regiment attached to the 18TH Hussars. In March of that year, they, like many thousands of other British soldiers, were engaged in a fighting retreat in the face of the German army's last attempt to win the war. Raymond was killed in action on 25TH March whilst fighting near Bernafay Wood, and buried in Carnoy Cemetery.[34] He was thirty-seven years old.

WILLIS Raymond of Cliff Cottage Seaford **Sussex** lieutenant 5th reserve cavalry attached 18th Hussars died 25 March 1918 in France Probate **London** 5 July to Emmie A'Court Allan Willis widow. Effects £55942 11s.

Announcement of the death of Raymond Willis, Cliff Cottage Seaford

---

[32] This information taken from Raymond's obituary in *The Times*, according to an article at http://www.epsomandewellhistoryexplorer.org.uk/WarMemorialsSurnamesW.html#WillisR

[33] Email from Nicholas Willis, great-nephew of Raymond. Nearly half a million volunteers joined up between 4TH August and 12TH September. The poet Rupert Brooke was amongst them claiming 'it will be hell to be in it and hell to be out of it.' Unlike Raymond, Rupert Brooke did not enlist as a 'private', but was given a commission in the navy.

[34] See Appendix 2 for account of how Raymond died.

On 22ND February, just one month before Raymond's death, Emmie had given birth to their first child, a son, also named Raymond. Like many other women of her generation, she had now become a widow with a small baby after barely a year of marriage. Raymond's will – witnessed by the manager of Lloyds Bank in Seaford on 13TH February 1917 – shows that his wife was the sole beneficiary, inheriting an estate valued at £55,942 at the time of his death. Emmie did not immediately sell the house, for *The Times* of 30TH August 1919 contained an advertisement for a 'cook, parlour maid and house-maid', with the instructions to 'apply Mrs Raymond Willis, Cliff Cottage, Seaford '. She is still registered as the occupant in the street directory of 1920–21, and in 1920 the name of Mrs Raymond Willis at Cliff Cottage appears in the British Phone Book, with the number Seaford 105.

By 1922 however, Emmie had taken the decision to move on, as the street directory of 1922-3 reveals that Cliff Cottage now had new occupants. Raymond's great-nephew has very fond memories of Raymond and Emmie's son, Raymond Willis junior, whom he describes as 'a wonderful man, much loved by all the family'. But he also tells how the young Raymond had grown up with little stability, being taken from hotel to hotel and spending some weeks each year with his relatives in Canada. His life, like those of so many of his contemporaries, had been hugely affected by the events of 1914-18. And if Raymond senior had returned safely to his family in Seaford at the end of the war, then the story of Cliff Cottage could also have been a very different one.

Car passengers enjoying a drive to Splash Point. Cliff Cottage is still unaltered from its original state, so this photograph is taken before 1924.
Courtesy of Seaford Museum

Enjoying a stroll on the seafront in the 1920s

CHAPTER 4

THE 1920s AND THE ADDINSELL FAMILY

After the end of the war in 1918, Seaford continued to attract visitors who wished to benefit from the healthy sea air, and the population rose with the influx of pupils who boarded at the growing number of private schools scattered around the town. Amongst those joining the residents of Seaford in the early 1920s were William and Annie Addinsell, who became the new owners of Cliff Cottage in 1922.

William Addinsell was born in Birmingham in 1859, the son of a Master Hosier. By the age of twenty-two he had become an 'accountant pupil', progressing to 'chartered accountant' by the time of the 1891 census, when he and his new wife Annie were recorded as living in Edgebaston together with one servant. There are no census records for the family for 1901, but 1911 finds them in London, living at the grandly titled Harrow Weald Lodge, with three servants: a nurse, a cook and a housemaid. The Addinsell family had grown considerably since 1891 and William and Annie now had four sons: Thomas (b 1892), Hugo (b 1894), John Edward (b 1896), and Richard (b 1904). Newspaper records reveal that William was a man who was interested in politics, as he is named as the defeated Liberal Candidate for the West Somerset constituency in the 1910 general election results.[35]

So what prompted the move to Seaford? William is listed as a member of the Seaford Links Golf Club in 1913, and would therefore have already been familiar not only with the town, but also with the house and its location. In 1922 he would have been sixty-three years old, so had perhaps decided to spend more time playing golf in Seaford's bracing air, whilst taking advantage of the excellent rail link to facilitate any business trips to London. William's financial interests now extended beyond accountancy, for by 1923 he was the chairman of the Sungei Kari Estate Company, which had owned rubber estates in Sumatra since 1909. William had been a director of the

---

[35] *Western Daily Press* – Tuesday 15 March 1910. William lost to the Conservative candidate by 368 votes (Cons 1,909, Lib 1,538).

company from the beginning – an astute move as the rubber industry at that time was about to go through a boom period, precipitated by the growth of the automobile industry.[36] The Electoral Register for the company's London address includes the names of both William and his wife, but interestingly lists their 'abode 'as 'Cliff Cottage, Seaford' for all the entries from 1922 to 1926, confirming that this was not just a holiday home.

The Addinsells had their own ideas – as well as the necessary funds – for developing the property. In 1924 plans were submitted by Seaford builders Messrs Green and Son for 'additions to Cliff Cottage', including a new dining room and the creation of another veranda – with 'porthole' windows – which considerably altered the appearance the sea-facing side of the building. Perhaps the Addinsells wished to create the impression that they were living on a ship, an image taken up by later holiday brochures which noted that the 'gardens and terraces are... right on the edge of the cliffs, and give one the impression that one is walking on the deck of a ship but without the consequences of mal de mar'.[37] The brick pillars and arches which still

Seaford from the Golf Links, posted in 1926. The card includes the message 'We have walked most of the way over here. It's a very nice place indeed'. William Addinsell , who owned the house during the 1920s, was registered as a member of the Links Club in 1913 so was perhaps attracted by the idea of living so close to the course.

[36] In *The Times* of July 19TH 1909 William is listed as a Director of the Company.
[37] Brochure of the Friendship Holidays Association 1932.

stand today at the Cliff Road entrance to the site could also have been part of William and Annie's improvement plans, as they are not present in the early photograph of the house shown on page 21. During the 1920s the house was not only given new porthole windows but also a new name: the Addinsells presumably considered the title 'Cliff Cottage' to be inappropriate for a house with nine bedrooms and by 1927 it had become Cliff House.

The couple's four sons were aged between eighteen and thirty-two when the Addinsells purchased Cliff Cottage in 1922. Shipping records from the 1920s show that their eldest son Thomas travelled to both South Africa and South America, and it is worth noting that the entries list his address in the United Kingdom as 'Cliff House, Seaford'– further proof that the house was not just a weekend retreat for the family.

The most well-known member of the Addinsell family, however, is William and Annie's youngest son, Richard. Richard had been educated at home – possibly due to the concerns of his over protective mother – and was eighteen years old when his parents moved to Cliff Cottage. In the same year he began a Law course at Hertford College Oxford, which he subsequently abandoned after only eighteen months. His interest was turning to music, and for a short period he studied at the Royal College of Music before once again rejecting formal education and instead honing his musical skills through working with composers such as Noel Gay, who was responsible for the music for *Me and My Girl*. By the 1940s Richard had become a famous composer himself, providing scores for such well known films as *Goodbye Mr Chips* (1939), *Gaslight* (1940), *Blithe Spirit* (1945), *Tom Brown's Schooldays* (1951), *Scrooge* (1951), *The Greengage Summer* (1961) and *Life at the Top* (1965). His most famous work is the *Warsaw Concerto*, a Rachmaninoff like piece for piano and orchestra composed for the film *Dangerous Moonlight* in 1941. Richard also extended his repertoire through his professional collaboration with the comedienne Joyce Grenfell, writing songs for her revue shows and often accompanying her on the piano.

Richard Addinsell composed the scores for many important films of the 40s, 50s and 60s including the soundtrack to 'Scrooge' starring Alastair Sim. His first work in British film was for The Amateur Gentleman (1936) which coincidentally was the film shown at the opening night of the Ritz cinema in Seaford.

A later owner of Cliff House – by then in its last phase as the 'Splash Point Hotel' – was fond of telling his guests that Richard Addinsell had composed the *Warsaw Concerto* whilst living there.[38] Sadly, this seems unlikely, as the *Warsaw Concerto* dates from 1941, thirteen years after the Addinsells had left Seaford and at a time when Cliff House was occupied by the army. But an eighteen-year-old who found it difficult to settle at university would surely spend time at the family home, and it is interesting to note that the list of the Fellows of the Zoological Society of London for 1924 includes the name Richard Stuart Addinsell Esq, with the address Cliff Cottage, Seaford. It is not too fanciful to picture the young composer developing his musical skills at the piano in the house on the cliff, with the sea in all its moods beyond the windows.

Richard Addinsell by Anthony Buckley 1949.
© estate of Kenneth Hughes / National Portrait Gallery, London.

[38] Two separate guests from the 1950s – Pat Stewart and Sally Culling – refer to this in letters sent to Seaford Museum. The owner at the time was William Gwyn Bowen.

CHAPTER 5

THE 1930s AND
THE FRIENDSHIP HOLIDAYS ASSOCIATION

In July 1928, property hunters searching for a new home may well have scrutinised the page of advertisments placed in *The Times* newspaper by the London based firm of Hampton and Son. Amongst the descriptions of country estates, stately homes and manor houses offered for sale by the company they would have seen the details of a 'beautifully placed freehold marine residence...in a glorious situation at the Eastern end of the Esplanade and commanding a magnificent panaromaic view in all directions'. The

Advertisement for the sale of Cliff House, from The Times, Tuesday July 3RD 1928.
The house was being sold by the Addinsell family, who had lived there during the 1920s.
The 'carriage drive' referred to in the advertisement was approached from Cliff Road, as there was no transport access from the promenade at this point.

Addinsells had decided to relocate to Chute Lodge, a grand house and estate near Andover in Hampshire, and a new chapter in the history of 'the house on the cliff' was about to begin.

'Cliff Cottage' had been standing for a mere thirty years, but this short period had been an eventful and turbulent time both for the inhabitants of the house and for the country as a whole. Maria Fleming Baxter would no doubt have approved of the fact that women over twenty-one now had the right to vote and were wearing knee length skirts; she would not, however, have been able to anticipate that ten years after her death the then owner of her seaside retreat would be numbered amongst the millions of casualties of one of the bloodiest conflicts in British history. By 1928 there were motor cars parked outside her house, and after 1920 the inhabitants had been able to communicate with the outside world by telephone. In their leisure time they could view 'moving pictures' at Seaford's Empire Cinema which was equipped to screen 'talkies' in 1930; six years later they may have attended the grand opening of the Ritz Cinema where they would have watched *The Amateur Gentleman* and heard the accompanying music, appropriately composed by former Cliff Cottage resident Richard Addinsell.

As we have seen, prior to 1930 Cliff Cottage had belonged to a succession of wealthy, well connected individuals. But times were changing, and it is significant that the new owner came from a far more humble background and was to use the house for a very different purpose. Cliff Cottage was no longer to be a private dwelling for the privileged few; it was now to become a business.

The Friendship Holidays Association

The inter-war years saw many people enjoying an annual holiday for the first time. Braggs and Harris, in their book *Seaside Holidays between the Wars*, note that by the end of the 1930s 'the annual holiday was the norm for fifteen million people', many of whom had secure jobs in the new industries of 'automobile manufacture, electricity and electrical goods and the service sector'.[39] There was money to be made from providing the British public with an enjoyable experience on their trips away from home, and when Billy Butlin opened his first camp in Skegness on Easter Saturday 1936 it was already fully booked for the season.

Henry White, the new owner of Cliff House, was another example of an entrepreneur who took advantage of this growing demand for low cost holidays. Henry had started his working life as a thirteen-year-old year old newsboy; six years later he was the manager at the WH Smith bookstall at Poulton-le-Fylde near Blackpool, where he remained for twenty years. One

[39] *Sun Fun and Crowds – Seaside Holidays between the Wars* Braggs and Harris Tempus Publishing Limited 2000.

day he noticed an advertisement in a newspaper for a boarding school which was to be let for the summer, complete with furniture and linen. Henry saw this as an opportunity to offer potential customers affordable summer holidays, and the Friendship Holidays Association was born. By 1931 the FHA brochure contained details of over twenty holiday centres where clients could stay, which included properties in Scotland, Wales, Devon, and of course Sussex.

Henry regarded Seaford – with its access to both Downs and Sea – as a very suitable location for the type of holiday he was offering, for the 1931 brochure offers a choice of two venues in this small coastal town. Current Seaford residents would not be familiar with the name of 'Queenwood', a 'wonderful house, right on the shore' which offered 'splendid bathing, tennis and a spacious ballroom', but the building in the accompanying photograph would be instantly recognisable as Corsica Hall, which at that time was a boarding school called Seaford College. 'Queenwood' followed the pattern of many of the buildings which Henry used, as it was rented by the FHA for the summer months when the school was closed.[40]

Cliff House, however, was a different proposition. It was one of the few properties which Henry White actually owned, and in the 1931 brochure is described as 'our permanent guest house'. Henry's granddaughter, Liz Brooking, tells how Henry was always on the lookout for a bargain, and

The above photograph of a motor charabanc was taken at an unidentified FHA property, but guests travelling to Seaford also had the option of being conveyed to their destination by this mode of transport. The man in the front is Henry White, the owner of the Friendship Holidays Association.
Reproduced with kind permission of Liz Brooking

---

[40]   Henry also rented Tyttenhanger Lodge and Kingsmead Schools in Seaford, renaming the latter 'Berners Court' in the brochure.

suspects that he may have picked up the house quite cheaply, possibly at the auction mentioned in the advertisement.[41] Henry himself would not have lived in the house as the business was based in Yorkshire; he would however have visited regularly on his tours around the centres.

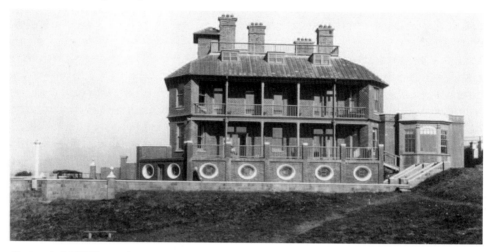

Postcard of Cliff House circa 1930 (above), when it belonged to the Friendship Holidays Association. The 'porthole windows' had been added by the Addinsells in 1924, as had the dining room on the right of the photograph. The windows in the roof are also a later addition.

The photograph below shows the site as it is today – the brick viewing area on the left and the boundary wall in the distance are both visible in the 1930s photo.

Hannah Rowsell photography

---

[41]   Email from Liz Brooking, granddaughter of FHA Founder Henry White.

A week at a Friendship Holidays Association centre would no doubt have been a more refined affair than a stay at Butlins, but there were some similarities between the two. Both gave holidaymakers an escape from their daily lives, relieving them from the chore of cooking meals and providing them with the opportunity to socialise with others. The large numbers who chose Butlins for their holiday would have been entertained by some of the stars of the day and encouraged to join in with the various communal activities on offer. At the FHA centres the guests themselves were responsible for providing the entertainment, taking part in 'impromptu concerts' in the evenings where volunteers who could play and sing were welcomed. 'Friendship' was the essence of the experience offered and FHA holidays were advertised as 'opportunities for adventure, for the healthy enjoyment of leisure, for shared experiences and the promotion of firm friendships'. The new relationships forged at the centres during the summer were revived at the autumn reunions organised by the Association, and Liz Brooking relates how many a match was made courtesy of the FHA, which was nicknamed the Find a Husband Association. Indeed, Henry's own daughter – Liz's mother – met her future husband at one of the centres.

centres.

Arriving on the Saturday afternoon the guests, young or not so young, married or " still looking," are met and welcomed to the week's House Party by the Host, Hostess or Centre Leader (the first two are on hand to " make it a party" in the evening, and the Leader, as the name implies, to lead the various walks, tramps, coach or steamer tours).

A welcome cup of tea and the guests are shown to their bedrooms. After a tour of the Common Room (known in hotels as the " Lounge," but in the Guest House more the scene for friendships to be fostered and strengthened as the week flies by), writing room, games room, dance room, they are left to unpacking while the officials repeat their duties until "all are safely gathered in."

By 5-30 p.m. nearly all the guests will have arrived and Saturday tea, a " sit-down " meal, is the switch that sets the week's activities in motion. At this meal and during the evening get-together social and dance, guests from places as far apart as Aberdeen and Plymouth become friends in a truly friendly party, and by 11 p.m., the customary end of organised evenings, all usually retire, tired perhaps, but looking forward to the first full day of their long-awaited holiday.

Sunday is a free day. Optional walks to local beauty spots under the Leader's guidance if required, with an evening in the Common Room perhaps, to sing, to exercise your intellect, or just to sit and listen to your fellow guests entertaining you.

The above passage describes the experience that holidaymakers could expect at the beginning of a FHA holiday.

Holiday photos Cliff House 1930

An official Friendship Holiday Association photograph showing a group of guests in front of Cliff House in July 1930. One of these guests – the lady third from the left in the second row – used her own camera to record her stay, and the results provide an interesting insight into a FHA holiday at Cliff House.

The photographs on pages 57 – 59 were taken with a camera belonging to the lady on the left of the first picture (entitled *Seaford July 1930*). As well as spending time on the beach, guests at Cliff House during this July holiday visited Litlington tea rooms, played tennis and dressed up in 'fancy dress', which apparently was the norm for 'Friday night' entertainment at a FHA establishment.

The captions are transcribed from the back of the photographs.

Seaford July 1930

*View of Seaford promenade July 1930
from Cliff House*

Ivy on Seaford Beach July 1930

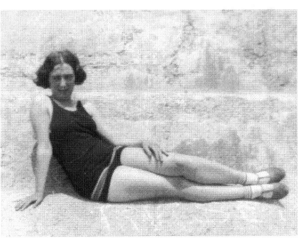

Seaford July 1930

'L.G' July 1930 Leonard Gilbert

*Ivy and self July 1930
Fancy Dress Cliff House*

Fancy Head Gear at Cliff House

*Litlington Tea Gardens
July 1930*

58

Litlington July 1930

Tennis Court at Seaford July 1930. The court was probably at Seaford College – now Corsica Hall.
The Martello Tower can be seen in the distance.

One of the main attractions of a holiday at Cliff House was undoubtedly the stunning location, which provided up to thirty guests with the opportunity to fully unwind during their week away from work. The brochure extols them to experience the fine air which 'speedily refreshes and renews weary bodies and tired nerves', making it 'a most desirable residence for those requiring a rest and the joys of the sea air and sunshine'.[42] Henry, like his predecessors, was clearly aware of the therapeutic nature of a stay at this house.

Staff from Cliff House in the early 1930s. The lady in the centre of the photograph is Jessie White, whose husband Henry owned the Friendship Holidays Association. Jessie died in 1933.

Staff and guests from Cliff House. One of the 'porthole windows' – added in the 1920s – can be seen on the right.

[42]   Summer Holidays with the FHA 1939.

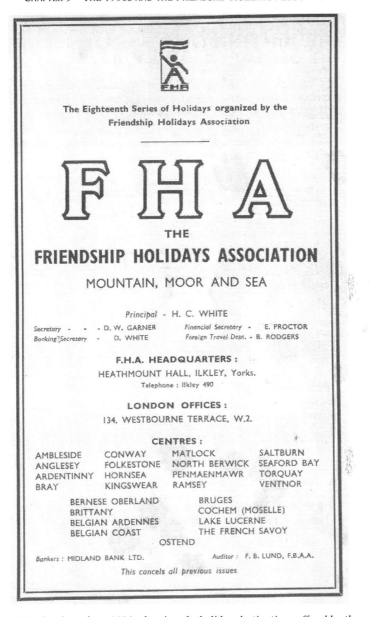

The Eighteenth Series of Holidays organized by the
Friendship Holidays Association

FHA

THE
FRIENDSHIP HOLIDAYS ASSOCIATION

MOUNTAIN, MOOR AND SEA

Principal - H. C. WHITE

Secretary - - - D. W. GARNER   Financial Secretary - E. PROCTOR
Booking Secretary - D. WHITE   Foreign Travel Dept. - B. RODGERS

F.H.A. HEADQUARTERS :
HEATHMOUNT HALL, ILKLEY, Yorks.
Telephone : Ilkley 490

LONDON OFFICES :
134, WESTBOURNE TERRACE, W.2.

CENTRES :

AMBLESIDE	CONWAY	MATLOCK	SALTBURN
ANGLESEY	FOLKESTONE	NORTH BERWICK	SEAFORD BAY
ARDENTINNY	HORNSEA	PENMAENMAWR	TORQUAY
BRAY	KINGSWEAR	RAMSEY	VENTNOR

BERNESE OBERLAND	BRUGES
BRITTANY	COCHEM (MOSELLE)
BELGIAN ARDENNES	LAKE LUCERNE
BELGIAN COAST	THE FRENCH SAVOY

OSTEND

Bankers : MIDLAND BANK LTD.   Auditor : F. B. LUND, F.B.A.A.

This cancels all previous issues

Page from the FHA brochure from 1939, showing the holiday destinations offered by the association including some situated on the continent. Prospective holidaymakers were politely reminded that they should expect certain differences if they ventured abroad: under the section entitled 'Notes on all Foreign Tours' Henry has written 'It should be emphasised that those booking on foreign tours will not find the conditions exactly the same as at our British Centres…one of the principal objects of a Continental Holiday is to mix with other nations than our own'.[43]

[43] Summer Holidays with the FHA.

SUSSEX

SEAFORD BAY. "Cliff House," right on Seaford Head, 12 miles from Eastbourne, is our permanent guest-house. Wonderful panorama from all windows. Its gardens and terraces are tastefully set out and are right on the edge of the cliffs, and give one the impression that one is walking on the deck of a ship, but without the consequences of mal-de-mer. It is most invigorating, and the tonic of its fine air speedily refreshes and renews weary bodies and tired nerves, making it most desirable for those requiring a rest and the joys of the sea air and sunshine. Seaford has a very fine promenade, stretching nearly to Newhaven, a distance of three miles. Splendid bathing, tennis, golf (links one minute), dancing. Seaford Head has been purchased by the National Trust. **Open April 9 onwards.**

CLIFF HOUSE.

Telephone : Seaford 650. Manageress : Miss H. M. Porter.

CHARGES. *Easter, 9/- per day.. From April 18 to May 30, 45/- per week. From May 30 to September 26, 63/- per week. From September 26 to December 19, 45/- per week.*
A few garden houses 50/- weekly.

EXCURSIONS.
  Weeks beginning - May 30 ; June 13, 27 ; July 11, 25 ; Aug. 8, 22 ; Sep. 5, 19.
    SEVEN SISTERS, LITLINGTON, WEST DEAN AND EXCEAT.
    BATTLE ABBEY, HASTINGS, AND PEVENSEY.
    FIRLE BEACON, ALCESTON, ALFRISTON, AND BERWICK.
    LEWES AND BIRD BROW.
  Weeks beginning - June 6, 20 ; July 4, 18 ; Aug. 1, 15, 29 ; Sep. 12.
    BEACHY HEAD, BIRLING GAP, AND EASTBOURNE.
    ARUNDEL, LITTLEHAMPTON, HOVE, AND BRIGHTON.
    WANNOCK GARDENS AND JEVINGTON.
    HINDOVER, CRADLE HILL, AND LULLINGTON.

Cost of excursions about 17/- each week.   *All excursions optional.*

24

Friendship Holidays Association Brochure from 1936. The manageress at the time is named as Miss H M Porter, who came from Manchester. Hilda Porter retained close links with the FHA, as her signature appears in the leather-bound book presented to Henry White on his eightieth birthday in 1955. see p 69.

Kindly provided by Liz Brooking

VIEW FROM CLIFF HOUSE

SEAFORD BAY
SUSSEX

" Cliff House," right on Seaford Head, 12 miles from Eastbourne, is our permanent guest-house. Wonderful panorama from all windows. Its gardens and terraces are right on the edge of the cliffs, and give one the impression that one is walking on the deck of a ship, but without the consequences of mal-de-mer. It is most invigorating, and the tonic of its fine air speedily refreshes and renews weary bodies and tired nerves, making it most desirable for those requiring a rest and the joys of the sea air and sunshine. Seaford has a very fine promenade, stretching nearly to Newhaven, a distance of three miles. Splendid bathing, dancing, public tennis courts, putting, boating, and golf (links one minute). Seaford Head has been purchased by the National Trust.

Open May 27 to September 30.

Telephone : Seaford 285011. Postal Address : " Cliff House," Seaford Bay, Sussex.

CHARGES.
  Whitsuntide 10s. 0d. per day (minimum 3 days).
  May 27 to July 22 63s. 0d. per week | Aug. 26 to Sept. 30 63s. 0d. per week
  July 22 to Aug. 26 70s. 0d. per week |

EXCURSIONS
Weeks beginning - May 27; June 10, 24; July 8, 22; August 5, 19; September 2, 16.
  BEACHY HEAD, BIRLING GAP, AND EASTBOURNE.
  ARUNDEL, LITTLEHAMPTON, HOVE, AND BRIGHTON.
  WANNOCK GARDENS AND JEVINGTON.
  HINDOVER, CRADLE HILL, AND LULLINGTON.

Weeks beginning - June 3, 17; July 1, 15, 29; August 12, 26; September 9, 23.
  SEVEN SISTERS, LITTLINGTON, WEST DEAN, AND EXEAT.
  BATTLE ABBEY, HASTINGS, AND PEVENSEY.
  FIRLE BEACON, ALCESTON, ALFRISTON, AND BERWICK.
  LEWES AND BIRD BROW.

Cost of excursions 20/- each week

All excursions optional

Page Eight

Friendship Holidays Association Brochure from 1939. The photograph provides an interesting view of the layout of the grounds of Cliff House.

The Friendship Holidays Association flourished throughout the 1930s, but as the decade drew to a close it was clear that things were about to change. Henry must have sensed that this was not a good time to be running a hotel, for in February 1939 he wrote to the council asking if they wished to purchase the plot for the price that he paid for it 'before it gets into the hands of speculative builders'.[44] The council did not take him up on his offer, and in November 1940 Henry sent a newsletter to his clients informing them that 'we have plenty of activities but they are not the kind we like…all our houses have been taken over by the Government'. The country was at war again, and the house in Seaford had been the second of Henry's properties to be commandeered. Henry ended the letter with the poignant words

> 'we are longing for the day when this great and tragic War will be over and we shall be able to open all our houses again in preparation for our guests, for it is the joy of meeting friends on holidays that helps us to get through our work during the rest of the year'.

For the next five years it would no longer be holidaymakers occupying Cliff House, but the British army.

---

[44]   Letter from Henry White to SUDC , 8TH February 1939 Held by The Keep, Brighton.

CHAPTER 6

CLIFF HOUSE: IN TIME OF WAR

Inevitably the events of 1939 and beyond had a huge impact on the seaside towns dotted along the channel coast. As the Germans advanced across Europe, the country began to prepare for invasion and Seaford once again began to fill with troops. R J Taylor, who was stationed in the town with the Royal Sussex Regiment from May to August 1940, recalled how things changed after the evacuation of Dunkirk in late May and early June. He had arrived in Seaford to take part in a driving and maintenance course, but was now given more pressing tasks including guard duty at the Martello Tower, where he witnessed German planes dropping mines in and around New-haven Harbour.[45]

The people of Seaford must have looked back wistfully to the summer of 1939 when easy access to the town's beaches was an accepted part of living by the seaside. Mr Taylor reports that despite the hot weather in the summer of 1940 'the beaches were out of bounds to everyone', for they were mined and the Esplanade covered with barbed wire to thwart any possible invasion by German landing craft. He describes how there were road blocks at various points around the town – such as at the railway bridge by the Buckle – which were manned twenty-four hours a day. The council minutes for the war years describe some of the effects of the large military presence in Seaford, including roads damaged by army vehicles, the use of the golf course for firing practice, and the accumulation of dust on the Eastbourne Road caused by the increase in traffic.

In November 1940 the Surrey Convalescent Home wrote to the Council asking for a reduction in their rates 'in view of the fact that the property has been earmarked by the government and no patients are in residence'. The large buildings which housed the convalescent homes and schools in Seaford provided an ideal base for the troops stationed in the town, and were there-

---

[45]   Letter from Mr Taylor courtesy of Seaford Museum.

fore requisitioned for use by the military. When searching for suitable properties the government must have been delighted to discover a hotel with panoramic views of the channel situated in a prime spot on Seaford Head, and Cliff House soon became one of the buildings under its control. The house even came with a ready-made observation post in the form of the brick 'viewing turret' – still standing today – which had been incorporated into the original wall. Peter Longstaff-Tyrrell includes a photograph of this turret in his book *Barracks to Bunkers,* arguing that 'the reinforced concrete roof platform and period brickwork suggest it became a lookout or light machine-gun post'.[46]

Brick observation turret which was part of the original wall. According to Peter Longstaff-Tyrrell (author of 'Barracks to Bunkers') the turret shows evidence of having been used as a lookout or machine-gun post during WW2.
Photograph reproduced with kind permission of Cliff Jones Photography © cliffjones

Plans were already in place to occupy the house by the end of 1939, for in November of that year FHA owner Henry White had applied for permission to erect a wooden building 'for storage of personal effects during the occupation of Cliff House by the military authority'. A temporary license was issued 'for a period of one year or for the duration of the war'.[47] Six months later R J Taylor was eating his meals in the house, for the building had now become a cookhouse for troops in Seaford. No longer was this the ideal spot for 'renewing weary bodies and tired nerves' as it had been in the days of the Friendship Holidays Association, for Mr Taylor tells how he watched a small

---

[46] *Barracks to Bunkers* by Peter Longstaff-Tyrrell Sutton Publishing Limited 2002.
[47] Copies of the plans are held at the Keep Records Centre.

coastal vessel explode – after hitting a mine – directly opposite where he was queuing for his lunch.

The residents and buildings of Seaford suffered considerably from the effects of enemy action during the war years, with twenty–three people losing their lives and a further hundred receiving injuries. Amongst the deaths was that of the Chief Air Raid Warden Mr W.P. Tomley, who was killed by German machine gunners as he made his way to the Control Room at Crouch House. Twenty-eight properties were totally destroyed and numerous others damaged, including fifty-four which were beyond repair and therefore demolished.[48]

Despite its prominent position Cliff House remained standing, although as we have already seen, plenty of wartime activity would have been witnessed from its windows. In October 1942 a Mrs P Womack had been posted to Seaford from a gun site near Portsmouth and billeted in a house near the golf course. Mrs Womack recalls how the radar set was positioned on the edge of the cliff 'next to a dummy gun site made of wood and sand-bag figures', while the real gun site was 'well camouflaged opposite the golf club house'.[49] She describes how one afternoon 'a German plane came over,

Matilda tanks of 44TH Royal Tank Regiment on the clifftops at Seaford Head, Sussex, 15 March 1941.
Image courtesy of Imperial War Museum©IWM (b8032)

[48] *The War in East Sussex*, published by the *Sussex Express 1945*.

[49] Letter from Mrs Womack courtesy of Seaford Museum. The council minutes of 17TH October 1946 also refer to the 'heavy gun site in the coppice opposite the Golf Club House', which the government eventually released from requisition in January 1947.

dropped a bomb on some shops then machine gunned the dummy gun site and radio set on its way out to sea'. It is likely that this was the enemy plane that was responsible for the most serious raid on Seaford on 25TH October 1942, when several people were killed including Warden Tomley.

Photographs of Cliff House taken in the late 1940s show that outwardly it had changed very little since the pre-war days of the Friendship Holidays Association, although the interior would undoubtedly have suffered from the years of army occupation and tread of soldiers' feet which caused damage to so many requisitioned buildings around the country. In June 1945 Miss Witherington of Seaford Ladies College wrote to the council 'regarding priority and sufficient labour being make available for the repair of schools which it was understood were now being derequisitioned by the military' [50] – a concern which would no doubt have been shared by the owners of the hotels in the town who would also have been keen to get back to business. After the end of the war the indomitable Henry White – now aged seventy-one – began to build up the Friendship Holidays Association again,[51] but Cliff House was no longer part of his plans and by 1948 had re-opened with new owners and a new name.

This photograph was taken on 12TH January 1949 in connection with the sea defence work being completed at the time. Note how much the cliff has eroded since the beginning of the century.

[50] SUDC minutes June 6TH 1945.

[51] Henry's business continued to survive until his death in 1961.

Henry's granddaughter tells how he never became rich because the holidays were inexpensive 'and every year there was a free guest week; poor families could be nominated to come and have a holiday free, albeit out of season.' On Henry's eightieth birthday in 1955 he was presented with a leather-bound book containing signatures of family and friends of the FHA, which bore the inscription 'He lives for the FHA and the FHA lives because of him.' His dedication to the organisation is indisputable, for he even insisted on having one particular brand of sausages – Palethorpes – 'sent to every guest house from the manufacturers in the Midlands, every week'.[52]

Henry White's background may have been very different to that of Maria Fleming Baxter, but they undoubtedly shared a strength of character and independence of mind that led them to purchase 'the house on the cliff'.

---

[52]   Email from Liz Brooking, Henry's granddaughter, July 2016.

CHAPTER 7

POST WAR – THE SPLASH POINT HOTEL

The Re-opening of the Hotel – Ronald and Helen Glover

As the war drew to a close, people who had not had a holiday for years wanted to make up for lost time and were eager to return to the beaches. In November 1944, Seaford Urban District Council were already planning for the following summer and recommended that 'the Beach Hut (at Dane Road), which had been used for the purpose of forming part of a military road block…be not sold but repaired and made available for the 1945 season'.[53] By February 1945 tenders were being invited for the beach huts and the cafe at the Salts; the War Office wrote to say that they had no objection to this 'provided of course all measures were taken that the council thought desirable to ensure the safety of the front users'.[54] The council recommended that notice boards should be erected along the promenade warning bathers and others against the possible danger of hidden steel tubing etc. A further reminder of Seaford's recent history was received during the storm of October 1945, when eight mines were washed ashore, including one which exploded at Splash Point.

The effects of the war could not be erased overnight, and the people of Seaford now faced a new battle, to restore and reinvigorate their town. In July 1946 the council resolved that the sites of bombed buildings in the centre of the town should be tidied up and 'available seats be placed thereon where possible'.[55] In February of the following year – over 18 months after VE day – the clerk to the council reported that there were still 900 Morrison and Anderson shelters in Seaford waiting to be collected. At this time the War Department continued to retain control of part of the Golf Course, and any-one in the vicinity of Cliff House would have seen notices warning of the

---

[53] SUDC Minutes 22ND November 1944.
[54] SUDC Minutes 2ND May 1944.
[55] SUDC Minutes 11TH July 1946.

presence of live ammunition on Seaford Head.[56] Cliff Road – which led to the house – was reported to be in a dangerous condition with the 'surface being crossed with deep ruts',[57] presumably a result of the years of heavy army traffic accessing the Head. Towards the end of the war Mr. L. A. Pearcy of Windy Knoll had written to the council complaining of the state of the road and declaring that as a protest he was 'withholding payment of his General Rates': the council presumably had more pressing problems to solve and informed him that 'Cliff Road is a private road and if repaired the cost would fall to be defrayed by the frontagers.'[58]

By spring 1947 the number of war-related items listed in the council minutes had at last begun to diminish and the focus shifted from the past to the future. Attracting visitors to the town became a new priority and in May 1947 a Mr. F W Thomas was approached 'on the matter of the production of an official guide to Seaford'. The rather dull pre-war publication was to be rewritten and updated with new photographs and a bright front cover, which

A new guidebook for Seaford with a colourful front cover was produced for the beginning of the 1948 season.

[56]   In 1960 – fifteen years after the end of the war – the Head of East Quinton School wrote to the council because his pupils were constantly finding abandoned war material, mostly 'mortar bombs, anti-tank bullets and 303 rounds'.

[57]   SUDC Minutes 10TH February 1947.

[58]   SUDC Minutes 13RD November 1944.

was 'to be in two colours and the design to incorporate the pictorial map of Seaford now in course of preparation' as well as the phrase 'Seaford for Sunshine'. The council members who were told of this slogan at the meeting of 11TH September 1947 may well have appreciated the irony when they also heard that the photographs for the guide had been delayed because 'the photographer …had not had satisfactory weather conditions for the subjects allocated to him'.

Six thousand copies of this new brochure were produced in time for the 1948 season, with local hotels and boarding houses being invited to submit an advertisement free of charge. In 1948 the population of Seaford was less than ten thousand, but the brochure contains more than thirty advertisements for hotels and guest houses of varying sizes. Visitors on a low budget could stay at one of the many small guest houses to be found in areas such as Claremont Road and Pelham Road; those wishing to opt for something more grand could book a room at the Esplanade Hotel on the seafront, or at Seaford House in Crouch Lane, which offered guests a walled garden, lawn tennis court and breakfast in bed.

Potential visitors to Seaford would also have noticed an advert for a newly opened establishment named the Splash Point Hotel, which 'adjoins Seaford Head Golf Course and commands an unrivalled position overlooking Seaford Bay and the Downs.' The name may have been unfamiliar but the description could only have applied to one property in Seaford – Mrs Fleming Baxter's house on Seaford Head, now entering a new phase as a post-war seaside hotel.

The advertisement includes a line drawing of the building from the Cliff Road side showing the sea on the right and the golf course on the left, and beneath the illustration appear the words 'newly opened under expert London Management', a rather grand description of the new owners of the property: Ronald and Helen Glover.

At the outbreak of war in 1939 both Helen and Ronald had indeed been registered as residing in London – although not yet at the same address – with Helen's occupation listed as 'Flats Manageress' and Ronald's as 'Building Construction Manager (previously Supervisor Aircraft Factory)'; both of which could be viewed as a useful background for anyone planning to own a hotel.[59] By 1946 they were living together as man and wife – with Helen using the surname Glover – at a house called Aylwards Lodge in Harrow East, although they did not actually marry until 7TH December 1948, when Ronald was forty-nine and Helen forty. Ronald's profession is described

---

[59] Information provided by 1939 register.

Advertisement for the newly opened Splash Point Hotel, which appeared in the 1948 'Seaford for Sunshine' brochure.

is a 'Company Director (Builders)'[60] on the marriage certificate; he is also listed as a 'widower' which could explain why the couple did not marry earlier.

It would appear that the hotel was already up and running prior to the ceremony, as Helen's address on the certificate is given as the Splash Point Hotel, Seaford. *The Dundee Courier* of 1ST November 1947 – almost a year before – had carried an advertisement for two young girls 'required to train as nannie and housemaid, very good home, wages and prospects', with interested applicants instructed to write to 'Mrs Glover, Splash Point Hotel, Seaford, Sussex'. Helen had grown up in Laurencekirk, Scotland – where her father had been an Estate Manager – which could explain why she chose to advertise in a Scottish newspaper. Around the same time Ronald had applied for a licence 'to sell intoxicating liquor for consumption either on or off the premises', an innovation which would not have gained the approval of previous owner Henry White, who was a Methodist and staunch teetotaller.

The Glovers would have been aware of the renewed demand for seaside holiday accommodation and, like Henry White twenty years earlier, probably thought that the unique location of the house on Seaford Head would attract the clients. Indeed, Sally Culling, who stayed at the hotel dur-

---

[60] In 1954 Ronald was writing his Splash Point Hotel letters on headed notepaper with the words Glover (C H and F London) Ltd at the top; the company had only two directors – R Leslie Glover (Managing Director) and H Glover M H C I.

ing her honeymoon in 1957, describes the setting as 'very Daphne Du Maurier, with the crashing of the waves on the beach below and the cry of the sea birds as they swooped over the cliffs.'[61] The town of Seaford itself was promoted as offering much to the holidaymaker, including 'Healing Peace, Healthy Exercise, Good Company, Tonic Air, Plenty of Sunshine and Soothing Scenery.'[62]

Rough sea near Splash Point. Listening to the sound of the waves – as described by guest Sally Culling – would have been a feature of any stay at the Splash Point Hotel.

The nearby cliffs often attracted film makers as well as tourists, and in August 1951 the hotel provided the accommodation for members of a film crew who were shooting scenes for David Lean's *The Sound Barrier* on Seaford Head. Director Lean and his then wife Ann Todd stayed at The Seaford Head Golf Club Hotel, but production manager John Palmer and assistant director Adrian Pryce-Jones were amongst eleven other members of the crew who were based at the Splash Point Hotel. The filming went well and John Palmer later wrote to the council to thank them for their help and co-operation, proclaiming that 'everyone is delighted with the results.'[63]

On occasions the hotel's cliff top location provided the setting for real-life dramas as well as fictional ones. In May 1949 hotel owner Ronald Glover was involved in the rescue of twelve-year-old Nevill Smith, who had become stranded on a narrow ledge fifty feet below the top of the cliff while collecting birds' eggs. The rope ladder lowered by Mr Glover was un-

---

[61]   Letter from Sally Culling April 2015.

[62]   *Seaford for Sunshine* brochure published by Seaford Urban District Council 1948.

[63]   Letter from John Palmer to SUDC 16TH August 1951, held by The Keep, Brighton.

fortunately too short, so Nevill remained on the ledge – two hundred feet above the rocks – while another rope was fed down to him. Nevill then tied the rope around his waist and was hauled up until he was able to reach the rope ladder, eventually arriving safely at the cliff top – shaken, but otherwise none the worse for his adventure.

Newspaper article from 1949 featuring the dramatic rescue of twelve-year-old Nevill Smith, who had become stranded fifty feet below the clifftop while collecting birds' eggs. The report describes how 'men from a nearby hotel lowered a rope ladder'.[64]

Courtesy of Seaford Museum

---

[64] The copy of this article in the Museum archives does not include a date, but the same story appears in *The Aberdeen Journal* of Monday May 9TH 1949.

Accidents also occurred lower down the Head, where the footpath that had been fenced off by Maria Fleming Baxter fifty years earlier was once again causing problems. The area between the boundary wall and the cliff face was now considerably eroded and in a dangerous condition, prompting the council to erect their own barbed wire fence and an accompanying warning notice in an attempt to prevent the public from using the path. It would appear however that these deterrents were often ignored, and in June 1951 Helen Glover wrote to the council to voice her concerns:

'I cannot emphasise too strongly how concerned I am about the cliff position generally, as my husband is constantly being called upon to help people who, through ignoring your notices and forcing their way through the barbed wire at the beginning of our red brick wall, get themselves into difficulties. As recently as Sunday (27TH May) in view of a crowd of people on the beach he went to a woman's aid – the ground had given way and she was slipping rapidly towards the edge and a sheer drop on to concrete below. No one else came forward to help – not even her companion who stood too terrified to move. A number of people came up from the beach afterwards to express their appreciation and admiration for what my husband had done, and said how dangerous it was and why was it that more effective measures were not taken by the council to prevent the risk of such a happening'.[65]

One such witness was Herbert Ponton of 55, Sloane Square SW1, who also wrote to the council to draw their attention to the incident, claiming that 'the woman would certainly have fallen if someone had not appeared with a rope ladder and hauled her to the top'.[66] The hotel's rope ladder was indeed an important piece of equipment; this could well have been the same one that had been used in the rescue of Nevill Smith two years earlier.

The Council's surveyor organised a subsequent inspection of the site, concluding that 'any person who had negotiated the protective fencing has only been able to do so with extreme difficulty and intent of purpose... I do not consider that the Council can do any more to stop people doing something if they are really determined to do so despite very reasonable and thorough precautions to stop them'.[67] No doubt many of today's local councils would empathise with this problem.

---

[65] Letter from Helen Glover to the Council 4TH June 1951, held by The Keep, Brighton. East Sussex Records Office DL/D 28

[66] Letter from Herbert Ponton to the Clerk to the Council 28TH May 1951.

[67] Letter from the Engineer and Surveyor to the Clerk of the Council 13TH June 1951.

Rear view of Cliff House from the 1930s.
Courtesy of the Rosemary Holland collection

*Postcard from the 1950s showing the view of Seaford Bay from the 'house on the cliff',
by now called the Splash Point Hotel .*

A New Owner – William Gwyn Bowen

Advertisements for the Splash Point Hotel appeared in the 'Seaford for Sunshine' brochures throughout the 1950s, with the text being supplemented with a drawing rather than with a photograph. In the early days this depicted the entrance to the building from Cliff Road, but by 1956 the brochure contained a different drawing, illustrating the more imposing view of the hotel from the promenade. The signature GLOVER can be seen in the bottom right hand corner; the artist could well have been either Ronald or Helen themselves. Photographs from the 1950s record another – more original – attempt to advertise the business, for they show how white stones were used to spell the word 'Hotel' on the grassy bank facing the promenade.

Photograph of the Splash Point Hotel showing how white stones were used to spell out the word 'Hotel' on the grassy bank.
Courtesy of Seaford Museum

Advertisement from The Seaford Guide 1959.

This photograph shows guest Sally Culling in the grounds of the Splash Point Hotel during her stay in May 1957. Sally remembers how the two parrots in the picture 'made an awful lot of noise' in the hall of the hotel.
Reproduced with kind permission of Sally Culling

The hotel held accounts with several local businesses, and deliveries were made to the kitchen via the path that ran past the left hand side of the building from the brick archway in Gerald Road. Rod Goodyear worked for various local stores as a schoolboy in the 1950s and remembers calling at the kitchen after school to deliver fish from MacFisheries, groceries from Winchesters in Church Street, and fruit and vegetables from Elizabeth's in Dane Road. Rod recalls how a 'large, very ornate parrot' was kept in a cage by the kitchen door, and describes how he and his friends would hide behind the fence in their free time and 'repeat swear words in the hope that the bird would mimic us'.[68] Parrots also feature in the memories of guest Sally Culling, who tells how 'two parrots who made an awful lot of noise lived in a large cage in the hall... {which was} dominated by the curvaceous staircase and large reception desk' – thus providing a tantalising image of the interior of the house.

Not everyone who traversed the path from Cliff Road was as bold as Rod Goodyear. A selection of personal recollections compiled by the Women's Institute[69] includes an account from a lady who grew up in Seaford in the late 1930s and retained vivid memories of her childhood fear of the red brick house on the cliff:

[68]   Email from Rod Goodyear October 2015.
[69]   *East Sussex Within Living Memory* – East Sussex Federation of Women's Institutes 1995.

Photograph of Seaford High Street from the 1950s. The shop on the right is MacFisheries, which provided fresh fish for the Splash Point Hotel.

'Nowadays you can approach Seaford Head from the seafront without fear of meeting the Giant, although the foundations of the house where I was sure he lived are still there.

When we strolled along past the jetty… and up on to the Head we had to pass the big red brick house and go through a narrow passage-way with a high wall on each side, into which there was a gate which gave access to the house.

My heart pounds now as I walk again the narrow aisle, my step quickens as I approach the gate and listen for the slightest sound. The enormous hinges would surely creak if the handle was turned…the gate might open and the Giant grab me inside'.

(See photograph on page 21 which shows the location of the passage-way referred to in this account, although the gate mentioned was not present at this time.)

At some point between 1955 and 1956 the business changed hands, for the minutes of the Seaford Urban District Council meetings for 1956-7 refer to the 'former owner 'and 'present owner' of the Splash Point Hotel. The Glovers remained in the Seaford area, moving firstly to Friston Lodge and then – in 1961 – to a house called Pilgrims in Borough Lane, Eastbourne, where the couple were still living at the time of Ronald's death in 1969.

The new owners of the Splash Point Hotel were William Gwyn Hughes Bowen and his wife Winifred, who had recently returned to the UK after time spent in West Africa. Shipping records show that in the immediate post war years the Gwyn Bowens regularly travelled to and from the Gold Coast, now known as Ghana, where William's occupation is variously described as 'clerk', 'secretary', and eventually 'accountant'. In December 1955 they arrived back in the UK for an 'indefinite' duration,[70] and by July of the following year were living at the Splash Point Hotel.

Running a business overlooking the sea in the quiet resort of Seaford must have provided quite a contrast to life in West Africa. According to the simple leaflet produced by the hotel at the time the catering was 'under the direct supervision of the resident proprietress' and there was a well-stocked wine cellar containing 'a wide selection of choice wines'.[71] It cost from 32s 6d to 40s per person per day to stay there including breakfast, lunch, dinner and baths – the more expensive rooms were presumably those with balconies.

The Gwyn Bowens soon discovered that owning a hotel on Seaford Head was not without its problems, and on 5TH July 1956 William wrote to the council complaining about the condition of Cliff Road and the Eastern Parade from the Cricketfield Road junction to Splash Point. Car ownership was increasing rapidly in the late 1950s and he would have wanted to make the entrances to the hotel more attractive and accessible for drivers. The Council agreed to consider the possible extension of the metalled surface from the Cricketfield Road junction to Splash Point 'when this Committee's estimates for the year 1957/58 are framed';[72] they were not, however, prepared to consent to the making up of Cliff Road when there were so many other potential road improvement schemes on their list.

In the following year William made another attempt to boost business by requesting permission to place an 8' x 4' sign – with the wording 'Splash Point Hotel/Open to Non-Residents' – on the wall near the Esplanade entrance to the site. Express consent was granted by the council on 15TH July 1957, but by this time the Gwyn Bowens were already making other plans.

[70]   The term 'indefinite' is used on the shipping record for their arrival from West Africa on 5TH December 1955.

[71]   The archives of Seaford Museum hold a photocopy of this leaflet.

[72]   SUDC Minutes 10TH September 1956.

CHAPTER 8

THE BEGINNING OF THE END

In September 1957 *The Times* carried an advertisement for the sale of 'An extremely well appointed Hotel on the Sussex Coast', with a 'superb position' on Seaford Head 'adjoining Golf Course and the cliffs with wonderful views across the Channel and the South Downs'. The Gwyn Bowens' foray into hotel management had lasted less than two years, and the Splash Point Hotel was on the market again, complete with all its contents.

Advertisement from The Times, Friday September 27TH 1957

The advertisement stressed the suitability of the building for 'School, Convalescent Home or similar purpose', suggesting that it was now struggling as a standard hotel. Sally Culling remembers how many of their fellow guests in May 1957 'all seemed very old to us, perhaps living there on a more permanent basis…not a retirement home but perhaps something along the lines of apartments for genteel retirees'. Another guest, Pat Stewart, recalled how one night, during a storm, William Gwyn Bowen was praying for lightning to strike the flag pole so that he could claim the insurance if the hotel burned down. As the 1950s drew to a close, the prospect of making a success of a hotel business in Seaford seemed far less likely than it had done in the immediate post war years. The rise of the private car meant that middle class families were no longer restricted to travelling to their holiday destinations by train and could be more flexible in their choice of location, leading to the growth of independent holidays such as camping and caravanning. John Walton, in his book *The British Seaside*, argues that 'after the immediate post-war adjustment period was over, road transport really came into its own ', noting that 'even in the four years between 1951 and 1955 the proportion of holiday journeys taken by train in Britain fell from forty-seven per cent (itself a sharp reduction from the pre-war figures) to thirty-seven per cent, marking the shape of things to come'.[73] Many of these new drivers heading to the seaside for their annual holiday would have been attracted by accommodation which provided 'easy parking', large car park', or 'garage',[74] something which was not offered by the Splash Point Hotel. The car was not the only mode of transport to affect the popularity of the post-war seaside holiday, for the 1950s also saw the introduction of the first air package tours to more southerly destinations, whose promise of guaranteed sunshine would soon lure large numbers of holiday-makers away from the traditional British resorts.

This photograph showing the Splash Point Hotel was probably taken in the early 1960s after it had closed, as the word 'Hotel' on the grassy bank is now becoming overgrown. Another interesting feature is the large number of parked cars visible in the picture.

---

[73]   *The British Seaside – Holidays and resorts in the twentieth century* by John K Walton pub. by Manchester University Press 2000.

[74]   These phrases are all taken from the advertisements for other hotels in the *Seaford for Sunshine* brochure.

Seaford seafront with the Splash Point Hotel just visible in the background.

In the late 1940s and early 1950s the SUDC minutes were full of references to the need to attract holidaymakers to the town, but the minutes from the early 1960s tell a very different story. Visitors were still aware of the attractions of Seaford, but most of them no longer wanted to spend their annual holiday in the town – they wanted to settle there permanently. The list of planning applications submitted to the council began to grow, as the property developers rushed to satisfy the demand for residential housing. The words 'flats' and 'bungalows' appear again and again in these applications, for many of the potential new residents were retirees heading to the coast in search of a peaceful, healthy location in which to spend their remaining years. This phenomenon was not restricted to Seaford alone, for John Walton observes that 'The 1960s ... saw a new wave of seaside retirement, reaching down to the lower-middle and upper-working classes, as bungalows proliferated around established resort cores in places like Bexhill, Clacton, Herne Bay and (less dramatically but still significantly) across a wide range of resorts and coastlines, most obviously in *south-east England* and on the Lancashire coast'[75] [my emphasis].

John Odam, in his book *Bygone Seaford*, notes how after 1961 'housing development exploded to engulf the outer reaches of the town and infill most of the precious breathing spaces within'.[76] Residential areas that were developed during the late 1950s and early to mid-1960s include the Hawth Hill Estate, the Golden Key Estate (off Hillside Avenue), the Chyngton Gardens extension, Richington Way, Blue Haze Avenue, Chyngton Way, Fairways Estate, Lullington Close, Quarry Lane, Valley Drive and many more. The private schools and convalescent homes began to disappear as they were sold off for development, amongst them Langham Court in Crooked Lane (formerly the Seaside Convalescent Home), the Surrey Convalescent Home, and schools such as Chesterton, Stoke House, Ashampstead, and Tyttenhanger Lodge. Seaford town centre itself was not immune from these changes, and several landmark buildings, including the Old Tree Inn and Talland House, were demolished in the 1960s to make way for something more modern.

In this climate of 'build, build, build' it was inevitable that the local hoteliers were also tempted to sell off their sites for profit rather than struggle in an ailing industry. The Connaught Hotel was replaced by flats; another casualty was the Crouchfield Hotel which was sold for development in 1963.[77] The closure of the Esplanade Hotel in 1966 was a considerable blow to Seaford's standing as a holiday resort and prompted the council to

---

[75] *The British Seaside – Holidays and Resorts in the Twentieth Century* by John K Walton pub. by Manchester University Press 2000.

[76] *Bygone Seaford* by John Odam pub. by Phillimore and Co Ltd 1990.

[77] The Constitutional Club was eventually build on this site.

discuss 'the loss of the hotel accommodation resulting from the closing of hotels and boarding houses over the past few years'. A letter was sent to the British Travel Association asking if they knew of 'any plans to provide new hotels in the district and for their observations generally on the future of the holiday trade in this area'. The reply was not very encouraging; the only information they could offer related to the construction of the new Mercury Motel at Bishopstone, which – with its deference to the rise of the motor car – was very different to the traditional seaside hotel and would not necessarily bring increased trade to the businesses of Seaford.

It is hardly surprising that the last owners of the Splash Point Hotel decided that it would be a better option to sell the building for development rather than to wait for the flag pole to be struck by lightning. On the 11TH February 1959 the council considered an application for the 'conversion of flats, Splash Point Hotel, Cliff Road' submitted by 'prospective purchaser' Mr J B Curry.

This was approved in principle, with the proviso that the applicant was 'to be advised that until further detail is available approval cannot be granted for a specific number of dwelling units'. The further detail emerged at the meeting of 14TH September 1959, when the council considered an application submitted by Mr Curry to convert the building into five self-contained flats. Again the application was approved, but 'subject to compliance with the requirements of the East Sussex County Fire Brigade'.

The days of the Mrs Fleming Baxter's 'cottage' may have been numbered by this time, but that did not prevent the building from receiving one last name change. Mr Curry – now seemingly the owner of the site – no longer referred to the building as the 'Splash Point Hotel' but as 'Cliff Court', a more stylish and appropriate name for a property expected to contain five flats. The hotel paraphernalia was no longer required, and local resident Ray French recalls how his parents purchased cotton sheets and monogrammed cutlery at the sale of contents that took place after the closure of the business.

It is possible that Mr Curry's plan failed to satisfy the East Sussex Fire Brigade, or perhaps he had decided that this option did not maximise the amount of profit to be made from the site. Whatever the reason, by the time Seaford Council met in November 1959, Mr Curry had abandoned his scheme to convert the existing building, and had put forward another, far more radical proposal. The hotel – now described as 'disused' – would be demolished, and replaced with blocks of flats and maisonettes. Astonishingly the minutes record the council's response to this drastic application in just one word – 'approved'.

CHAPTER 9

FLATS ON SEAFORD HEAD?

Today it is hard to believe that permission could ever have been granted to build blocks of flats on Seaford Head. An article in the *Evening Argus* of 29TH December 1960 – entitled 'Council Answer the Beauty Spot Grumble' – reveals that the council was criticised for its failure to purchase the property, thus handing over the 'one remaining beauty spot' on the 'devastated front at Seaford' to speculators who would make a huge profit.[78] Chairman of the Council Mr H W Andrew responded to these complaints by stating that he 'did not think that the citizens of Seaford would have borne [the] burden 'of the £10,000 to £15,000 price tag. Thirty years earlier the council had purchased the bulk of Seaford Head – 'to preserve the area for the public as an open space'[79] – for a sum of £16,500, but on this occasion part of the cost was offset by the income generated from the golf links. Mr Andrew's comment implies that the council of 1960 felt that the acquisition of the remainder of Seaford Head was not something that could be financed by the ratepayers alone. The reaction of local residents to this decision are not documented, but those who wished to protect the natural heritage of the town must have feared that the familiar view of the cliff at Seaford would now be changed forever.

---

[78] *Evening Argus* 29TH December 1960 (courtesy of Seaford Museum). The site had possibly been sold on by Mr Curry, who had acquired planning permission in November 1959.

[79] *The Times* Wednesday November 16TH 1927.

EVENING ARGUS, 29/12/60 15

COUNCIL ANSWER THE BEAUTY SPOT GRUMBLE

'We did preserve Seaford Head'

CRITICISMS of Seaford Urban Council for their failure to buy the old Splash Point Hotel at the foot of the town's famous beauty spot, Seaford Head, were answered at last night's meeting of the council.

The criticisms were that the "one remaining beauty spot" on the devastated front at Seaford had been "handed over" by the council and that speculators had bought the hotel and, with planning permission for 42 flats and 30 garages, would be making a huge profit.

Council chairman Mr. H. W. Andrew said the council had fully discussed the matter. If there had been planning control 30 or 40 years ago an hotel would probably not have been allowed on that spot. Since 1900 at least there had been a building known as the Splash Point Hotel.

The suggestion was that the council should have bought the land, but it would have cost £10,000 to £15,000 and he did not think the citizens of Seaford would have borne that burden. The height of the flats to be erected on the site was considerably lower than the existing building.

'Out of question'

"I quite agree that the front would be nicer if there was an open space at the foot of the Head, but that is out of the question. We

● Seaford Head with the Seven Sisters in the background

In December 1960 the council had to answer criticisms as to why they had allowed the Splash Point Hotel to be purchased by property developers.
Article courtesy of the archives of Seaford Museum

By the following summer the people of Seaford were able to view an artist's impression of how the area at Splash Point might look if the flats were built. This drawing appeared in the sales brochure advertising the auction of the 'Valuable Freehold Site, known as Cliff Court, Cliff Road, Seaford, for residential development', to take place at the Terminus Hotel on 14TH July 1961 'by the direction of the owner'. The site was being sold on again, together with outline planning permission for a three-storey block containing eighteen flats on the site of the hotel building, with a further two-storey block of twelve flats to be situated further down the slope. By this time garages were an important consideration in any planning application; thirty of these were to be located behind the flats near the footpath at the end of Cliff Road. Twelve maisonettes, also with garages, would be built at the base of the slope, where the eastern end of Cliff Close is situated today.

SALES BY AUCTION

By the direction of the Owner.

SEAFORD—SUSSEX
VALUABLE FREEHOLD SITE

known as

CLIFF COURT, CLIFF ROAD, SEAFORD

of approximately 3.16 Acres

for

RESIDENTIAL DEVELOPMENT

Outline planning permissions have been granted for 30 Flats and Garages and 12 Maisonettes and Garages. Situated within about ¾ mile of Seaford Station and Town Centre in a magnificent position high up on the edge of the Downs with beautiful and extensive views over sea and countryside and with own separate private Drive down to the Esplanade and Beach.

FOR SALE by AUCTION as a WHOLE or in TWO LOTS

(Unless previously sold by Private Treaty) at the TERMINUS HOTEL, SEAFORD on FRIDAY, JULY 14th, 1961, at 3 p.m. precisely.

Subject to Conditions of Sale to be then produced and read which include covenants restricting user to private residences and usual appurtenances but which are believed to be obsolete. These Conditions may be inspected at the Offices of the Solicitors or the Auctioneer.

Particulars and Conditions of Sale may be obtained from the solicitors, Messrs. Moxon & Barker, Ropergate, Pontefract, Yorks, Tel.: 3215, or from the Auctioneer, Mr. W. G. F. SWAYNE, F.A.I., 3, Clinton Place, Seaford, Tel.: 2144.

Sale details for 'Cliff Court' (formerly the Splash Point Hotel). Advertisement from The Times, Wednesday June 14TH 1961.

BY THE DIRECTION OF THE OWNER.

Seaford, Sussex
VALUABLE FREEHOLD SITE

KNOWN AS

Cliff Court, Cliff Road, Seaford

FOR

RESIDENTIAL DEVELOPMENT

Outline planning permissions have been granted for

30 FLATS & GARAGES and 12 MAISONETTES & GARAGES

FOR SALE BY AUCTION at

THE TERMINUS HOTEL, SEAFORD

on FRIDAY, 14th JULY, 1961
(Unless previously sold by Private Treaty)
AT THREE P.M. PRECISELY.

Subject to Conditions of Sale which include covenants restricting user to private residences and usual appurtenances but which are believed to be obsolete. These Conditions may be inspected at the Offices of the Solicitors or the Auctioneer.

Solicitors:	*Auctioneer:*
Messrs. MOXON & BARKER,	MR. W. G. F. SWAYNE, F.A.I.,
49 Ropergate, Pontefract, Yorks. (Tel. 3215).	3 Clinton Place, Seaford Sussex. (Tel. 2144).

Front page of the sale brochure for the auction of 'Cliff Court' in July 1961.
Courtesy of Seaford Museum

An enlarged view of the artist's drawing showing the proposed development of the site of Cliff Cottage. The topmost block – to be built on the site of the original house – was to have three storeys and contain eighteen flats. Thirty garages – interestingly not visible in this drawing – were also to be erected between the flats and the houses in Gerald Road.

Courtesy of Seaford Museum

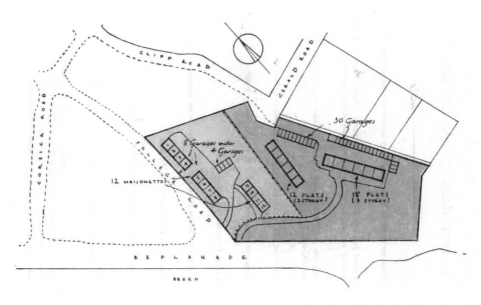

The above plan from the 1961 sale brochure shows the proposed location of the blocks of flats (in red) and maisonettes (in blue). The combined footprint of the flats and garages would have been far greater than that of the original house.

See page 92. Both images courtesy of Seaford Museum

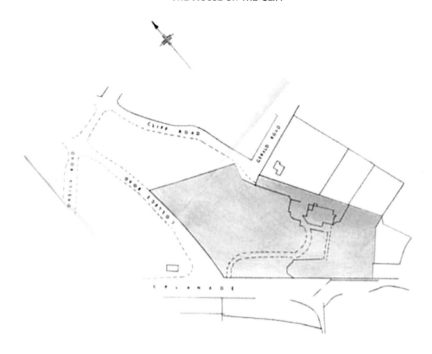

Three years later the blocks of flats pictured in the 1961 brochure had yet to materialise and the view from the promenade towards Seaford Head remained unchanged. In June 1964 the site was up for sale once again, with the same description but with the vendor now listed as Thomas Richard Reginald King, from Southern Ireland. The conditions of sale stated that 'completion shall take place ...on or before the 16TH day of June 1964 when *vacant possession of the property* [my emphasis] shall be given to the purchaser', indicating that the hotel was still standing at this point. The council had been sent the sale particulars in May but once again failed to seize the opportunity to acquire the plot, which was purchased by yet another development company with an eye on the potential offered by this unique location.

In 1960 Council Chairman Mr Andrew had argued that the height of the flats to be erected on the site was considerably lower than that of the existing building, but anyone acquainted with Seaford gales must have had wondered how modern blocks of flats would fare in such an exposed spot. Perhaps the latest developers had doubts themselves, for in December 1964 they presented the council with a new proposition, which they hoped would provide a satisfactory outcome for both parties. At that time the council owned the piece of land lying between Cliff Road and the extension of College Road, where the houses in Cliff Gardens and the western end of Cliff Close now stand. The developers enquired as to whether the council would exchange this piece of land in return for 'a strip of land lying between the proposed development and the cliff edge at Splash Point …for use as an open space'. This strip of land was defined at the March 1965 meeting as 'the major part of the former Cliff Court site lying between the cliff edge and the public footpath leading from Cliff Road'. The council presumably welcomed this opportunity to appease their critics by claiming back the foot of Seaford Head without having to find the money to pay for it. The developers found themselves in a good bargaining position; they were able to stipulate that they would agree to the terms of the exchange 'provided planning permission for the development of the land to be transferred to them is forthcoming'.

When following the account of these negotiations in the council minutes it is easy to overlook a crucial piece of information embedded in the detail. The developers refer to the land that they were offering to exchange as the 'former Cliff Court site'. It would appear that Mrs Fleming Baxter's house, which had dominated the slopes of Seaford Head for over sixty years, had now been demolished.

CHAPTER 10

THE SITE TODAY

It is now well over a hundred years since Cliff Cottage was first built, and the Seaford of today is a very different place to the sleepy seaside town with a population of two thousand that was frequented by Maria Fleming Baxter and her family in the late 1800s. Many of the Victorian buildings that characterised the seafront have gone, including the Esplanade and the Eversley Hotels, the latter – by then known as the Beachcomber – being demolished to make way for a McCarthy and Stone development in 2014. The base of Seaford Head is now skirted by the forty-three houses in Cliff Close and Cliff Gardens which were eventually built by developers as the 'Marina Estate' in the late 1960s and early 1970s, several years after the exchange of land with the council had taken place.

And yet in spite of these changes the seafront at Seaford continues to exercise its charm, and on sunny days families still flock to the promenade, where they cycle, picnic and paddle in the sea just as they would have done in Victorian times. If they climb the grassy slopes at the foot of Seaford Head they will see evidence that a house once stood there – the tall pillars and arch-ways that flank the footpath leading from Cliff Road, and of course that distinctive brick wall with its now crumbling tower which has weathered so many storms. Cliff Cottage itself may not have survived long enough to become a listed building, but we should be thankful that the council of the mid 1960s listened to the protests of Seaford residents, and found a way of preserving the site of Mrs Fleming Baxter's house for the people of the town. Today it is not concrete and tarmac that cover the ground but grass and wild flowers, and residents and visitors alike are still free to cross this open space as they make their way up Seaford Head. The small seating area – situated directly in front of what would have been the entrance to the house – is the perfect spot for admiring the spectacular views of Seaford Bay while listening to the sound of the waves on the shingle below. And for anyone acquainted with the history of 'the house on the cliff', it is still possible to feel a link with those people – the Victorian lady and her solicitor friend, the First

World War lieutenant, the composer, the entrepreneur, the soldiers of the 1940s and the hoteliers of the 1950s – whose lives were touched by this special place.

The plans for 'Marina Estate', the houses in Cliff Gardens and Cliff Close which were eventually built at the base of Seaford Head.
Courtesy of Seaford Museum

Aerial photographs showing the site today. If the development plans of the 1960s had gone ahead the green area shown in the picture would have been the site of thirty flats and thirty garages.

Photographs reproduced with the kind permission of Peter Fellows

Boundary wall beside the footpath from Cliff Road.
Photo provided by Hannah Rowsell Photography

Author's Note sent via email on 29/9/16

The last few pages of John Odam's book *Bygone Seaford* – published twenty-five years ago – contain photographs of buildings in Seaford which the author felt should be preserved as 'Our Present Link with the Past'. I have decided to conclude *The House on the Cliff* in the same way, and the final pages of this book feature photographs of the remains of Cliff Cottage that are still visible today. They may only be walls, pillars and arches, but they too provide a link to the past, adding a sense of atmosphere to the site and inspiring curiosity about its history. I hope very much that they are allowed to remain, and that in twenty-five years' time, visitors to Seaford Museum will still be asking the question: 'What is that brick wall on Seaford Head?'.

These brick pillars and archways marked the entrance to the grounds of Cliff Cottage from Cliff Road. They were not present during the time of the original owner Maria Fleming Baxter so were added later, probably during the 1920s. Thirty garages would have been built on this grassy path if plans to develop the site in the 1960s had gone ahead.

Photos provided by Hannah Rowsell Photography

*The remains of the boundary walls of the grounds of Cliff Cottage
provide a visible link to Seaford's past.*
Photos provided by Hannah Rowsell Photography

The red brick wall – originally built by Maria Fleming Baxter to define the seaward boundary of the grounds of her cottage – has withstood Seaford's gales for over a century, and volunteers at Seaford Museum still receive many questions from visitors curious to learn more about its history.

Photos provided by Hannah Rowsell Photography

APPENDIX 1

DATING and ANALYSIS OF PHOTOGRAPHS
OF MARIA FLEMING BAXTER

Professional dress historian and picture specialist Jayne Shrimpton has produced a detailed analysis of both the miniature portrait of Maria Fleming Baxter on page 7, and the photograph of Maria and her two daughters on page 8. Jayne's reports provide a fascinating insight into the creation of Victorian portraits and the fashions of the time, and I am grateful that she has allowed me to include her work in this book.

Miniature portrait of Maria Fleming Baxter (p7)
– an analysis by Jayne Shrimpton (extract only)
Usually accurate dating of images rests on dating the fashion details, but here Maria is not wearing contemporary modes, but has dressed up in 'fancy dress' costume suggesting the styles of the past. The Victorians deeply admired historical revivals in the decorative arts and accordingly for 'fancy balls', fashionable by the 1870s, many ladies devised picturesque costumes loosely based on Renaissance, Elizabethan or Tudor styles. Here Maria wears a 16TH-century style costume complete with high standing 'Medici' collar and puffed and slashed sleeves – features that may not be precisely dated but effectively convey an impression of Tudor, Elizabethan or Renaissance fashions. Her hair may have been artificially lightened and specially dressed in tight curls too, so that she somewhat resembles Queen Elizabeth I. Possibly she intended to represent that English monarch, although other historical figures were popular too, such as 'The Queen of Spain', whose costume was similar.

So, to conclude, Maria seems to have commissioned a miniature portrait that would have been very much in keeping with her contrived 16TH-century appearance in this picture. Dating broadly to c.1870-1880, perhaps you will be able to link her costume to a particular event that occurred around this time, such as a pageant or 'fancy ball.'

Photograph of Maria Fleming Baxter and her two daughters (p8) – an analysis by Jayne Shrimpton (whole report)

This is a beautiful portrait taken by a professional photographer. Since it is framed, we cannot see the original photograph in its entirety: the card mount may bear printed details of the studio on the reverse. The photographer could, as you suggest, be a well-known – possibly London-based – practitioner, or might be more local to Seaford (perhaps one of the more prestigious Brighton studios?) if the subjects were then resident in East Sussex. The setting is likely to be the interior of the studio, although it could possibly be the drawing room of the subjects' own house. Clients could request a representative from a local photography business to visit them at home, although in the early 1870s location work was a complex undertaking involving the transportation of much equipment and would have been an expensive option.

You have identified the lady as Maria Fleming Baxter and the fact that she hailed from a prosperous family is evident from the lavish coloured re-touching of the entire scene: this was probably executed by hand using watercolour paints and would have added significantly to the cost of the photograph. The colours seen here were almost certainly copied from life, offering a rare view of the shades in vogue for furnishings and, more interestingly, women's and children's clothing in the mid-Victorian era. Subjects usually wore their best, most fashionable garments when sitting for a formal photograph, aiding close dating, particularly of female portraits. You believe that the photograph dates to 1871 and this is a perfect year for Maria's dress and coiffure.

Female fashion was very elaborate during the early 1870s, especially among the wealthy who could afford the finest materials and profuse trimmings on their clothes. Maria wears a rich day gown comprising a hip-length over-dress layered over a matching skirt, the fullness of fabric behind her waist indicating the bustle projection, fashionable c.1870-75. The flattering pale gold silk fabric of her costume is set off by bands of minute pleating on the sleeves and hem of her over-dress and arranged in complex tiers down the skirt – a popular form of luxury ornamentation in the early-1870s: so, too, was the fringing just glimpsed on the back drapery of the over-dress. Another key dating feature is Maria's distinctive hairstyle. Echoing the exuberant, feminine dress styles, coiffures of the early-mid 1870s could be very intricate. Hair was drawn off the face and dressed in a high chignon that often involved plaited sections, as here: frequently artificial hair pieces were added to the natural tresses, to achieve this and similar heavy, decorative modes. Since the ears were revealed with such hairstyles, long pendant ear-rings also became fashionable at this time and Maria wears what look to be high quality gold and possibly jewelled drop earrings.

Maria's children are exquisitely dressed in good, fashionable garments suited to their respective ages, the colours of which blend in pleasingly with their mother's outfit and with the room furnishings. Stripy stockings were especially fashionable for little girls during the late 1860s and early-mid 1870s, so clearly Maria dressed her daughters in the latest styles. I don't see anything unconventional as such in her appearance, but, clearly, she was a lady who enjoyed spending money and displaying the latest modes. In this sense, we might infer that she was comfortable with drawing attention to herself – a tendency that could suggest a strong woman who others would notice and remember.

Jayne Shrimpton
www.jayneshrimpton.co.uk

APPENDIX 2

The website http://www.epsomandewellhistoryexplorer.org.uk/ provides the following detailed account of how Raymond Willis – an owner of Cliff Cottage – lost his life while fighting in France in March 1918.

The following is an extract from the *Memoirs of the 18TH Royal Hussars (Queen Mary's Own) 1906-1922* by Brigadier-General Charles Burnett, C.B., C.M.G. 24th March 1918.

March 24TH – At 5 a.m. on March 24TH the Regiment moved via Chauines, Vauxvillers and Proyart to Cappy, arriving there at noon. This movement to the north took place on the Division receiving orders to support the 39TH Division just south of the River Somme, and if necessary to cross the river at Feulleres and support the 21ST Division north of the river. The Headquarters of the 1ST Cavalry Division were at Mericourt, south of the Somme.

A party of 6 Officers and 160 other ranks, under Lieut. MacIlwaine, was sent to the Camoy Valley, north of the river, for employment in the trenches near Bernefay Wood. This force was heavily engaged during the evening of the 23RD and the night of 23RD-24TH, and lost Lieut. Willis and 9 other ranks killed, 2ND Lieut. Williams and 26 other ranks wounded; 7 other ranks were missing. At 12.30 p.m. this dismounted party was sent to support the right of the of the 21ST Division, and at 4.30 p.m. was ordered to fill a gap which had occurred between the left of the 9TH Division and the right of the VTH Corps in the direction of Trones Wood.

The remainder of the Regiment moved from Cappy to Cerisy at 8 p.m. and bivouaced there for the night.

March 25th – Early on March 25TH the Regiment, with the 2ND Cavalry Brigade, withdrew to Bussy-les-Deours, and halted there during the day with one troop on picquet duty on the Pont Noyelles Road.

Camoy was a front line village held by the British in 1916, and was the starting point for many British soldiers on 1 July 1916, the first day of the Battle of the Somme.

Raymond is buried in Carnoy Military Cemetery. He is commemorated on the Lloyds of London memorial outside their building in Lime Street and on his parents' grave in St Mary's churchyard, Ewell.

Seaford War Memorial also includes the name of **R Willis** amongst those who died in the 1914-18 war.

The website http://www.roll-of-honour.com/Sussex/Seaford.html cites that there is 'no further information currently available' on R Willis, so perhaps this was also a tribute to the Raymond Willis who lived at Cliff Cottage.

THE HOUSE ON THE CLIFF
TIMELINE 1897-1965

Date	Event
1897 – July	Edward Hammond, builder, submits the planning application to build Cliff Cottage for Maria Fleming Baxter.
1899	The name Mrs Fleming Baxter, Cliff Cottage appears in Kelly's street directory for Seaford.
1900 – September	The wall of Cliff Cottage can be seen in the photograph of the Norwegian ship Sagatun, which was wrecked on Seaford beach.
1901 – census	The occupants of Cliff Cottage are listed as housekeeper Emily Legget (58), parlour maid Violet Blake (16), and kitchen-maid domestic Lily Blake (15). Maria and Herbert Fleming Baxter are registered at their London home.
1905 – July	Herbert Fleming Baxter dies at Sibdon Castle aged 65.
1907 – February	Maria Fleming Baxter dies at Sibdon Castle aged 60. Edward Freeland inherits Cliff Cottage.
1911 – census	The occupants of Cliff Cottage are listed as caretaker Frederick Castle (35) and his wife Nellie (31). Edward Freeland is registered at an address in Kensington, London.

1916	Raymond Willis becomes the new owner of Cliff Cottage. He marries Emmie A Court Allan Cassells in January 1917.
1918 – March	Raymond Willis killed in action in France. His wife Emmie remains at Cliff Cottage.
1920	The name of Mrs Raymond Willis, Cliff Cottage appears in the British phone book, with the number Seaford 105.
1922	William and Annie Addinsell are now the owners of Cliff Cottage. The name of W A Addinsell Esq. appears in the street directory for 1922-3.
1924	Plans submitted for 'additions to Cliff Cottage' including a new dining room and the creation of another veranda with porthole windows.
c1927	Cliff Cottage is re-named Cliff House.
1928 – July	Cliff House is up for sale.
1931-1939	Cliff House – now owned by Henry White – is advertised as a holiday destination in the brochures of the Friendship Holidays Association.
1939 – November	Henry White applies for permission to erect a wooden building 'for storage of personal effects during the occupation of Cliff House by the military authority'.
1940	Cliff House has become a cookhouse for the army.
1947	The Splash Point Hotel is opened by new owners Ronald and Helen Glover.
1956	The Glovers sell the Splash Point Hotel to William Gwyn Bowen.
1957 – September	The Splash Point Hotel is advertised for sale in *The Times*.
1959 – February	'Prospective purchaser' Mr J B Curry submits an outline

planning application for 'conversion of flats, Splash
Point Hotel'.

1959 – September   Mr Curry submits a planning application to convert the
building – now called Cliff Court – into five self-
contained flats.

1959 – November   Mr Curry puts forward an application to demolish the
'disused' hotel and replace it with blocks of flats and
maisonettes. Application approved.

1960 – December   *The Evening Argus* reports that Seaford Council had been
criticised for their failure to purchase the hotel.

1961 – July   Cliff Court up for sale – by the direction of an unnamed
owner – with outline planning permission for 30 flats
and garages, as well as 12 maisonettes and garages.

1964 – June   Site advertised for sale again with vendor listed as
Thomas Richard Reginald King from Southern Ireland.
The words 'vacant possession of property' are included
in the conditions of sale, confirming the hotel is still
standing at this point.

1964 – December   New developers – Haron Development Co. Ltd,
Ringmer – enquire as to whether the council would be
prepared to negotiate an exchange of land.

1965 – March   Land to be exchanged referred to as 'the major part of
the *former* Cliff Court site [my emphasis]', implying that
the building has now been demolished.

1965 – April   Exchange of land agreed by the council. This allows
them to become the owners of the Cliff Court (formerly
Splash Point Hotel) site.

c1965   A photograph taken by Francis Frith Photography
confirms that the hotel is no longer standing on
Seaford Head.

ACKNOWLEDGEMENTS

The journey of this book first began in the autumn of 2011 when I joined the 'Seaford Rediscovered' course at Seaford Museum, where David Swaysland and Kevin Gordon inspired me to turn what had previously been a mild curiosity about the origins of the Splash Point Hotel into a full-scale research project. David and Kevin are just two of the many volunteers who dedicate their time to the museum in order that this wonderful treasure trove of all things Seaford can exist, and I would like to thank all the other members who have passed on suggestions and snippets of information. A special mention must go to Phil Armstrong for his help with the scanning of the images – several of which were provided courtesy of the Museum – and Peter Fellows who kindly took the aerial photographs of the site of the original house. Thanks are also due to IDM properties, Hancock's Jewellers, the Hampstead Heath website, Rosemary Holland, Chris Jones Photography, Phillip Mann Estate Agents, Jayne Shrimpton, and the Shropshire Archaeological and Historical Society, who have all allowed me to reproduce their materials in the book, and to architectural historian Clare Sherriff, who assisted with the section on Arnold Mitchell. I am also very grateful to photographer Hannah Rowsell, who took the evocative photographs of the present-day remains of the building.

I would like to acknowledge the help provided by the staff of The Keep at Falmer – another invaluable source of archive material – who patiently brought me copies of planning applications and endless volumes of council minutes. The discovery that I could view the original plans of the house was a defining moment in the early days of my research, and underlined the importance of this facility to anyone with an interest in the past. The website of the Epsom and Ewell Local and Family History Centre – run by volunteers – was another useful source of information, which helped greatly with the writing of the chapter on Raymond Willis.

I am indebted to many other people whose contributions have enabled me to piece together the 'jigsaw' of the story of the house. Rod Goodyear, Sally Culling and Nevill Smith provided interesting personal accounts of the 'Splash Point Hotel' era while Ann Griffiths, Janette Wells and Nicolas Willis kindly passed on knowledge about family members who had a connection to the house in earlier days. A very special 'thank you' must go to Teresa Sladen (great- granddaughter of Maria Fleming Baxter) and to Liz Brooking (granddaughter of Henry White), who not only provided key information relating to these two fascinating characters but also generously shared their wonderful photographs, which have added so much to the book. Their enthusiasm for the project and willingness to help has been much appreciated.

One of the best decisions I made was to hand over the production of the publication to Dick Richardson of Country Books, and I would like to thank him for the patient way in which he has transformed my text, illustrations and footnotes into a real book.

And finally I would like to thank my family for their encouragement and practical support – in the form of proof-reading, IT trouble-shooting, site-visiting, postcard-buying and coffee-making – and for sharing our home with the occupants of the 'house of the cliff' for the past five years.

BIBLIOGRAPHY

Baines, F E, *Records of the Manor, Parish, and Borough of Hampstead, in the county of London, to December 31ST, 1889*, published 1890

Ballin, Ada S, *The Science of Dress in Theory and Practice*, 1885

Banks, W, *Seaford: Past and Present. Handbook and Visitors' Guide, 1890-91*

Black's Guide to Sussex and its Watering Places, Eleventh Edition, Adam and Charles Black, London 1898

Braggs, Steven, and Harris, Diane, *Sun, Fun and Crowds – Seaside Holidays between the Wars*, Tempus Publishing Limited, 2000

East Sussex Federation of Women's Institutes, *East Sussex Within Living Memory*, Countryside Books, 1995

Gordon, Kevin, *Seaford Through Time*, Amberley Publishing, 2010

Longstaff-Tyrrell, Peter, *Barracks to Bunkers*, Sutton Publishing Limited 2002

Middlesex Victoria County History Committee, *A History of the County of Middlesex Volume 9, Hampstead, Paddington*, Victoria County History,1989

Odam, John, *Bygone Seaford*, Phillimore & Co. Ltd, 1990

Odam, John, (In association with Brigid Chapman) *The Seaford Story 1000-2000 AD*, S B Publications, 1999

Seaford Timeline, Seaford Museum and Heritage Society, 2002

Sherriff, Clare, *Arnold Mitchell (1863-1944): 'Fecundity' and 'Versatility' in an Early Twentieth-Century Architect*, SAHGB Publications Limited 2012

Walsh, John H, *Seaford Golf Club – A History 1887-1986*, Lindel Publicity and Promotions Ltd., 1986

Walton, John K, *The British Seaside: Holidays and Resorts in the Twentieth Century* Manchester University Press 2000

The War in East Sussex, published by the *Sussex Express*, August 1945

Newspapers and Brochures

Assorted archive newspapers were accessed through http://www.britishnewspaperarchive.co.uk/

Specific publications are referenced within the main text.

Archive editions of *The Times* were accessed via the East Sussex County Libraries website.

Country Life Magazine, June 1967.

Friendship Holidays Association Brochures (various editions from the 1930s).

Seaford for Sunshine Brochures, published by Seaford Urban District Council (various editions from the 1940s, 50s and 60s).

INDEX

78, 80-83, 86, 107-109
Splash Point,
Seaford Head
1, 3, 70, 81, 88, 93

T

Tower, The, (Fitzjohns
Avenue, Hampstead)
10, 11

V

Victoria Cross 4
Victoria, Queen 4, 10

W

Westover Hall 18
White, Henry 52-53,
66, 68-69, 73, 107, 110

Willis, Raymond 43, 44, 104